"Without being preachy or prescriptive, this book is loaded with practical insights that Tricia Williford seamlessly embeds within her charming storytelling. Tricia provides inspiration through authenticity by never shrinking from pain or hyping success. *Let's Pretend We're Normal* is an honest look at the often messy, sometimes joyful, and always loving work of being a family."

—JOHN COTTON RICHMOND, human-trafficking prosecutor and former director of International Justice Mission's slavery work in India

"Don't miss this one! Tricia Williford, a young widow with boys to raise, writes with honesty and humor about mining the beauty of life after 'happily ever after' meets 'I never saw this coming.'"

—SHELLIE RUSHING TOMLINSON, author of *Heart Wide Open: Trading Mundane Faith for an Exuberant Life with Jesus*

"Tricia Williford has found a way to sort through her grief, find treasures in the darkness, and then articulate it all in a way that's tangible and life-giving for those still in the valley. *Let's Pretend We're Normal* gives you an inside look at the everydayness of a family still finding their ~~way~~ after a significant loss. If you find yourself sorting through ~~~~ ~~~~ ~~~~ ~~~~ ~~~~agedy, you'll find a new friend ~~~~ ~~~~ gh her loss with honesty and he~~~~

—SUSIE LARSON, ~~~~ *Your Beautiful Purpose*

let's pretend we're normal

ALSO BY TRICIA LOTT WILLIFORD

And Life Comes Back

Tricia Lott Williford

let's pretend we're normal

Adventures in Rediscovering How to Be a Family

18868

WATERBROOK
PRESS

Let's Pretend We're Normal
Published by WaterBrook Press
12265 Oracle Boulevard, Suite 200
Colorado Springs, Colorado 80921

Details in some anecdotes and stories have been changed to protect the identities of the persons involved.

Trade Paperback ISBN 978-0-307-73200-2
eBook ISBN 978-0-307-73201-9

Cover design by Kelly L. Howard

Published in the United States by WaterBrook Multnomah, an imprint of the Crown Publishing Group, a division of Penguin Random House LLC, New York.

WATERBROOK and its deer colophon are registered trademarks of Penguin Random House LLC.

Library of Congress Cataloging-in-Publication Data
Lott Williford, Tricia.
    Let's pretend we're normal : adventures in rediscovering how to be a family / Tricia Lott Williford. — First Edition.
        pages cm
    ISBN 978-0-307-73200-2 — ISBN 978-0-307-73201-9 (electronic) 1. Families—Religious aspects—Christianity. 2. Families—Religious life. I. Title.
    BT707.7.L68 2015
    248.8'6—dc23

                                                          2014043263

Printed in the United States of America
2015—First Edition

10 9 8 7 6 5 4 3 2 1

For my mom and dad

You make me happy when skies are gray.

contents

prologue

Once upon a time there was a Curly Girl. When she was in college, she fell in love with Mr. Responsible, and they were engaged to be married just three months after they met, even though Curly Girl still can't believe anyone approved that engagement at age nineteen, because who were these kids kidding that they knew all about love? Anyway, Curly Girl turned twenty-one on their honeymoon, and this couple started a lovely—albeit young!—life together.

Curly Girl and Mr. Responsible had two children: Athlete and Artist. Athlete and Artist were born accomplices; in perpetuity, one had an idea, the other agreed, and the instigator could almost never be identified with complete accuracy.

For almost four thousand days, Curly Girl and Mr. Responsible lived the complicated, beautiful life of marriage. They woke up next to each other and kissed each other good night. They were honest and dishonest and unfiltered and guarded. They were kind and unkind to each other, often in the same day and somehow all at the same time. They took each other for granted, which is one of the hidden gifts of life together: the forgetting to appreciate. He took care of her in ways she didn't know; she brought color to his life in shades he didn't recognize. He was measured and careful; she was spontaneous and impulsive. He held the string to her kite; she was the air in his balloon.

Mr. Responsible died, suddenly and tragically. He was sick for only twelve hours. Doctors thought he had the flu. Nobody knew that he had an infection in his bloodstream and had become toxic to himself. A thief named sepsis stole his breath and his heartbeat, and his spirit slipped right through Curly Girl's fingers, even as she tried to save him on the floor of their bedroom only two days before Christmas.

In the course of one day, Curly Girl became the widowed, single mom of two children not yet in kindergarten. She lost her husband, her confidence, and nearly her faith. Curly Girl's world became very small, and she began to piece together a broken life one meal and one word at a time. Her two boys, Athlete and Artist, learned too much too soon: death is real, a parent can die, sometimes God says no, and heaven is a place that isn't here. They saved their mother's life by giving her a reason to live at all. A family of four became a trio, a braided cord with frayed edges but a tight knot.

Some stories finish with "And they all lived happily ever after." Other stories continue to write themselves. Scars don't go away, but life grows deeper than the scars and reveals a landscape that includes them. Boys grow taller, hearts grow stronger, the sun still shines, and life comes back. The opposite of death is creating, and an end can be followed only by a beginning. Curly Girl, Athlete, and Artist are living with joy and staying in the moment with a smattering of cake batter, finger paints, soccer practice, and unmade beds.

They're making it up as they go and rediscovering how to be a family, one adventure at a time.

Part One

"i will do this!"

one

When the worst thing you feared has happened to you, you can fool yourself into thinking you're out of the woods for any other tragic loss. You can tell yourself you've done your time, you went through hell and survived, and lightning surely won't strike the same family twice. This little white lie can help you begin to live again. This invincibility can give you the courage to do small things, like step out of your home or go to the grocery store or sleep at night. You might even begin to lean on this sense of security and start to try bigger things—like driving to a new city. Or taking your children on a hike in the mountains.

Sometimes the facade of safety is the biggest risk of all.

We live in Colorado, where the options for hikes and bike rides and day trips are endless. I mean, really, it begins to feel like poor stewardship if you don't get out and do stuff. I feel as if I shouldn't even get to live here if I'm not going to enjoy the sunshine and the thin air, as if someone might revoke my citizenship if I don't show my appreciation for this recreation mecca. With all this in mind, I decided to prove my courage, independence, and worth in Colorado by taking my boys on a hike.

I chose an "easy hike." Not a "big-deal hike." And certainly nothing that required equipment of any kind. In a book about hikes where they rate them from easy to hard with one to four stars, this route would get a half star. Rather than choosing to climb a mountain, I chose a path that would take us down through a craggy ravine right on the edge of a golf course. I took my phone and some sunscreen, and we set out to make a memory.

The experts on young men say that boys need a beauty to win and a battle to fight, and I assure you that taking their mom into the wilderness fit the bill on many levels. My guys felt—and acted—like the fearless duo of Indiana Jones and Buzz Lightyear. In their surge of masculine confidence, they asked if they could hike on their own for just a while, for just a little way.

Remember that sense of invincibility? It's not always your friend. For example, in this moment it would have been smart to say, "I love this great idea, guys, and while I totally believe in you and applaud your crazy courage, I'll go ahead and stay with you everywhere we go today."

But I didn't say that, because I was riding the wave of invincibility.

Together we chose a picnic table where I would sit and wait for them. I always have a book with me and zero qualms about having a few more minutes to read. I promised not to move so they could be sure to find me again, and they promised to stay together so I could be sure this wasn't the worst idea ever. See, while the downside of having boys less than two years apart is the fact that they each have a built-in accomplice to break any rule, the upside is that they also have a built-in bodyguard and teammate for any adventure. I could send them off together with the knowledge that one would truly lay down his life for the other. Or at least lay some serious threats against anyone or anything that threatened to come between the two brothers. So you can imagine my alarm when Tucker, the oldest at age nine, came back by himself. This was not the agreement.

Tucker didn't speak at all until he was three years old, and he and I worked long and hard in those early years to find his voice and vocabulary. So in the face of a trauma, the first thing that goes are his words. It's as though an emergency raises the drawbridge between his brain and his mouth. While he is keenly aware of everything happening around him, he is frozen in speechlessness. He cannot tell his side of the story.

This is particularly problematic when he's involved in any kind of altercation with a child in the neighborhood or on the playground. When a teacher questions the boys on what happened, there stands my silent child, who is strong and smart, a gentle giant just like his dad, without words to explain why he pushed a bully.

On that warm afternoon on the craggy cliff, he stood before me with his pleading eyes, and all he could offer for explanation was his brother's name.

"Tyler. Tyler. Mommy . . . Tyler."

Even though I knew he didn't have the words, and even though I knew he was saying everything he could say, my instinct begged for more information, and I peppered him with questions. "Where is Tyler? Is he okay? What happened? Tell me, Tuck. Tell me. It's okay, buddy. Show me. Just show me."

He took my hand and led me along the path they had followed. But before long one rock looked just like another, and we were lost. I could hear Tyler's cries echoing through the small canyon, but I couldn't find him. I called to him, "I'm coming, Tyler! I will find you, buddy!" I could only hope he could hear me.

Tuck and I climbed over giant rocks, lowering ourselves farther and farther into the canyon, following the sounds of Tyler's crying voice calling for me. Let me tell you, it was one of those times when the objective was so clear and my mind was focused on one task, but my thoughts unfolded into a dozen questions.

Should I call 911? Should I at least call my parents? But I'm losing my cell-phone signal, so if I am going to call, I have to stop climbing long enough to make a phone call, and I can't stop trying to find him for even one second. What if I get trapped where he is and I can't get help? Should I call for help before I lose my phone signal? How would anyone even find us if I can't find my own son? I wonder if they would send a helicopter down here for us. What if we are stranded in this stupid canyon for days? What if we are left to spend the night with the mountain lions? I have to find my child.

Hell hath no fury like a mother concerned, and a mama bear will literally scale a mountain to find and protect her red-headed cub. I would later look back on it all and be impressed with my own clarity—and upper-body strength. I spotted the very top of his marigold head—this was a moment when I was most thankful for his vibrant orange-red hair—far, far down the canyon. I made a beeline for him, scrambling as fast and as hard as a city girl can climb downhill over giant boulders. When I finally got close to my son, I still couldn't reach him; he had climbed onto a small ledge that was only wide enough for his two feet. I lay down on my stomach and stretched my Go-Go-Gadget arms over the side to reach his hands.

I lifted Tyler over the rock and into my arms. I scooped Tucker into the huddle, and together we caught our breath. As I held him and soothed him, hikers gathered around us. It turns out they too had followed the cries of the little boy. When you see strangers who are sweating because they want to help you rescue your child, it's enough to restore your faith in humanity. They gave us just a moment to hold on to one another and feel the solid ground beneath our feet.

Now that the three of us were together again, the story unfolded, and I learned what had happened. In my theory of safety in numbers, I had neglected to factor in the variable of disagreement. There's a tension between the compliant one who follows the rules and the creative one who tests the boundaries. I have one who likes to play it safe and obey, and I have one who likes to see just how far he can bend the rules without actually disobeying. Tucker felt they had ventured far enough, and Tyler wanted to go farther. Tucker remembered the rule to stay together, so he continued to follow his brother lower and lower into the canyon. Though he felt that it would be safer to stop, his brother felt plenty safe to keep going. In my experience, when a strong-willed younger sibling has the opportunity to take the lead, he's going to. Every time. So Tyler led the two of them right down the side of the canyon.

I needed to take a deep breath and regroup. In my fear I was looking for someone to blame and some consequences to enforce, but then I realized nobody had actually disobeyed or done anything wrong. It was just a classic dilemma of curiosity taking a boy a bit too far. We climbed back to safety together, and my adrenaline level began to ease down. The boys, resilient as they are, found their adventurous spirit almost right away. They were climbing, jumping, and skipping, and I was trudging along behind them in silence. I just wanted to get everybody back to the car and, quite frankly, teleported all the way home.

Tyler asked, "Mommy, why aren't you happy? Where is your joy? I thought you would be happy because I am safe."

"I am very, very happy that you are safe."

"Well, you don't *seem* very happy."

I stopped and brought the two explorers near me. "Listen. When you were afraid, you were able simply to be afraid. But when I was afraid, I couldn't let myself feel just that emotion. I had to choose to be brave and to think so I could rescue you. I couldn't sit down and cry and feel afraid, even though I was terrified that you were hurt or that I had lost you forever. You're okay now, and I know that. My spirit is very, very thankful that you are okay. But my mind has to catch up, Tyler. I need time to feel all the things you felt while you were afraid."

Also, my love, consider this to be a free lesson in the class called "Inside a Girl's Mind." Don't rush my emotions.

"Okay, Mommy. I'll give you time."

They scampered ahead with the sure feet of a couple of deer. I walked behind them, chastising myself for thinking we were strong enough, brave enough, wilderness-aware enough to go on this simple hike in the first place. *What were you thinking, Tricia? This was Robb's realm. Hikes, nature, outdoors, and boy adventures— those were his domain. Go ahead and put a red X on the checklist of*

*things you've tried, and now take it off the list of things you'll ever do
again. You can't do this. Adventure is not yours.*

I am prone to making hasty judgments with extreme statements like that. It wasn't until later that I could gain a different
perspective. Actually, I *had* braved the hike. I could, and I did.
We made it through the adventure, and I had learned something
more about my sons and myself. Instead of crossing this off the list
of things I will ever do again, perhaps I could file it under the
category of things I can and might do just a little bit differently. In
the face of the emergency, I had been able to *stay calm,* to *step up*
as my children needed me to, to *keep from putting anyone at risk,*
and to *live to tell about it.*

I realized that's kind of a four-step guide for this entire
journey—and maybe any journey at all.

Stay calm.

Step up as needed.

Don't put anyone at risk.

Live to tell about it.

So when the people who make books asked me to write a book
about parenting, I held up one finger in dispute, both to say "Hold
on one minute, please; let's not get ahead of ourselves" and "Let
me start with one solid reason why I should not write a book on
parenting: I don't know what I'm doing."

Understand, I'm playing this whole gig one day at a time. I
make a million mistakes, and I'm not sure you should do this the
way I'm doing it. My kids live on a balanced diet of technology

and Lunchables. I love them with my whole heart, and I am a walking mess most of the time. For crying out loud, just this morning I found a pair of my socks outside in the flower bed, the heels worn through in crusty holes, because my son wears my socks when he rides his skateboard. And when I say he "rides his skateboard," I mean that he sits on it to ride down the sidewalk, and when he needs to slow down, he brakes with his feet—the shoeless feet that are wearing my socks.

I am learning as I go. And aren't we all? Aren't parents just kids who grew up and had kids? What on earth would make me an expert to speak into anyone else's life about how to run this marathon? So, will I write a book on parenting? No, not if it's a book that prescribes how to be a better parent.

Which brings me to another reason and a second finger to raise in my argument. I think one of the heavier burdens I could give my children is my own book on how to parent. Then they might grow up under a microscope, under close inspection of a world watching to see if they indeed are maturing into men of integrity and leaders in their family and community. I sincerely pray every day that they become such leaders, but that's not what this book is about. Actually, I'm not sure their outcome as men of integrity has a whole lot to do with who I am as their mom, so I don't claim much business in writing about it.

And then the book people rephrased the question. "Tricia, will you tell some stories about your journey as a mom?" Aha. Storytelling. Now, this—*this*—I can do. And that's how we got here, with you holding a book written by a young widow who is just trying to keep up with her kids.

So don't worry: I won't try to advise you on how to raise your kids. God knows all too well that I'm barely managing to figure that out myself. But I will do what I do—tell stories upon stories of what I have learned from real life in the trenches, life as I know it in many seasons: married or single; taking a paycheck or working at home; and doing my time in this parenting club, where we never take a day off, we work extra hours on holidays, we catch chewed food as it comes out of a child's mouth, and we eat our own meals over the kitchen sink.

A friend said to me not too long ago, "Tricia, you do realize this is your life, right? It's not just a story—this is your life." It's true. I'm living the story, and I don't know how it ends. I don't create; I notice. I watch and I learn, and then I write it down. And so this is a book of the many things I have noticed along this path—from my first days as a single parent, when I had no idea how I would survive one day on my own, when I could do only the next thing, adding minutes to hours and meals to days. I want to tell you about learning the secret to gentle confidence, rediscovering how to be a family, and finally looking in the rearview mirror and saying aloud to myself and my guys, "You know what? I think we're doing this. I think we're going to make it."

If you're okay with the honest and up-front caveat that I'm learning as I go, that I'm only pretending to be normal, then grab a flashlight and join me. And hold on tight. This gig is a bumpy road.

two

This is my life.

The alarm goes off at 6:45, which is at best a suggestion, considering I never get up then. I'm a snoozer, which I think is the most natural way to be, since the Snooze button is the largest one on any alarm clock and deserves the most attention. I can fall back to sleep with no trouble at all, so the tinkling scales on my iPhone alarm are just a whisper of a wake-up call. In my sleeping mind I'm going right back to sleep until I hear it again. Long about 7:45, after an hour of giving myself "just ten more minutes," I get up.

Tyler, age seven, is already awake and watching cartoons at the table. Scattered around him are a smattering of Go-Gurt wrappers, since he's been munching his way through the morning. And I'm thankful for the person who invented yogurt in a tube, because I secretly think she had me in mind . . . or at least my son—pickiest of the picky eaters—who will snip open half a dozen Go-Gurts and carry them like a bouquet. As long as there are Go-Gurts in the fridge, then one part of Tyler's day will go well. Lately he's even been calling it "good luck," as if this feast hasn't a single thing to do with my grocery list.

I come downstairs to find him in his Spider-Man jammies, the ones that actually have this mesh webbing underneath the arms that makes him feel invincible. He has been working on his "all about me" poster for "student of the week." I see that he's completed it in purple Sharpie. Everything about this poster will be very purple and very permanent. I ruffle his hair. "Good morning, buddy."

"Good morning, Mommy. I don't have any nose hairs. Not any."

"You probably do." I kiss his noggin as I look over his shoulder to see the family portrait he has drawn on the poster. Next to the space for the family, there is a question: How many people are in your family? Instead of a number Tyler has written an equation: $4 - 1 = 3$. He's right. There were four. Take away one. Now there are three.

He has drawn a stick-figure Tyler, a stick-figure Tucker, a stick-figure Mommy with flippy hair, and a skeleton in the ground next to a gravestone that says RIP.

Halloween is coming; Target is inundated with candy corn, vampires, spider webs, tombstones, and skeletons; and my son has woven this into the picture of our family. In purple Sharpie.

Oh, honey. I want to scoop him up and remind him that our story is not a Halloween scene, his dad is not a ghost in a grave, and this is really not how I'd like for him to depict our family. But the story belongs to my son as much as it belongs to me, and Tyler is learning to tell it as he understands it. This is one of the challenges of childhood loss: as his cognitive abilities deepen, his understanding of the facts change. Death changes for him as he discovers more and more about life.

"Mommy, is a spleen a private part?"

I don't have to wonder what prompted the question. Tyler knows that Robb had his spleen removed after a sledding accident when he was fifteen. The spleen's job is to fight strep and staph infections, so Robb didn't stand a chance against the septic infection that flooded his bloodstream. He didn't have a spleen, and that eventually took his life.

I kneel down to answer Tyler, rubbing small circles on the back of his jammies. "No, honey. It's not. Your spleen is like your stomach or your kidneys—it's tucked inside your body. You can't see it, and you can't touch it, but it's not a private part."

"Oh . . ." The purple Sharpie hovers over the page. My son pauses.

"Why did you ask, buddy?"

"Because I think . . . Well, it's possible I might have told some people that my dad died because somebody cut off his private parts."

"No, you didn't. Please tell me you didn't."

"I did."

"Honey, who did you tell?"

"Well, I told Meghan because she sits right beside me. And then I told everyone who sits at my table. And then I told my whole class."

"You told your *whole class*?" *Oh my goodness.*

"I did. I told them that we don't really like to talk about it, and I asked them not to ask you about it if they see you."

So let me get this straight. My son told the entire second-grade community that my husband died because someone cut off his private parts, and he told them not to verify this information with me? I pictured the scene unfolding in the classroom and my son the center of attention with this golden fabrication that would have everyone talking. And I could only imagine how many children in his class took that story home to their dinner tables and now how many families wondered about "the official cause of death" but didn't feel comfortable bringing it up since Tyler had said it's something we don't like to talk about.

I held my forehead in my hands, wrapping my mind around the magnitude of it all. I would have been horrified except that it was all so terrifically funny. I could picture Robb's response. "Well, I'd *rather* die than have that happen to me."

"Mommy? Can we just leave it this way? I don't want to go back and fix it with everybody."

"No, no, I don't think we can let this one go, buddy." I don't know what I'm going to do, but I can't let this little rumor weed grow.

Tucker comes to the top of the stairs, dressed for the day even while he's still rubbing the sleep sand out of his eyes. He asks me where his socks are, and I direct him to a basket of languishing laundry that is clean but not folded or put away. We just fish things out as needed until the basket's empty, and then I'll do more laundry and not put it away again, and the cycle will repeat itself indefinitely.

Tuck will come down and fix my cup of coffee, a task he is most proud of. He has it all figured out: ten ounces of water in the orange mug that is my favorite, one container of decaf in the Keurig coffee maker, and then the perfect amount of creamer, because he has learned the brew's color that reveals a cup perfectly to my liking. He knows the Keurig inside and out, and I'm thankful for the person who invented it, since I'm sure she had me in

mind . . . or at least my son, who thrives when he is in charge, responsible, and taking care of someone. These qualities make him
very much like his dad. Actually, that pretty much describes
Tucker in a few words: he is all things Robb in every single way.
So of course he would learn to make a drink he's never tasted—if
it's what I love the most. And of course it is important to him to
get it right every time.

I let the dog out and ask Tyler to please get dressed. I offer
breakfast options. On a good day this might be muffins and Cap'n
Crunch and grapes. On a more typical day, this is frozen waffles
with Kroger syrup from a bottle with a sticky cap. No matter
what—*no matter what*—Tyler will not like the choices. I will ask
him to please try something new, just as I ask him at every meal.
He could subsist on Easy Mac and Go-Gurt. Sometimes I let him,
thinking it's just not worth the battle. But then I think of a friend
of mine who married and then learned that the only thing her
husband would eat for dinner was a cheeseburger and french fries.
She wanted to fix other dishes, but he wouldn't ever eat anything
different. So she had this newlywed battle in front of her, and she
wondered why his mother hadn't insisted on a little broader diet.

Well, surely I can't be that mom who never asked just a little
bit more. So on any given morning, I offer Ty other things, but he
settles in with the Go-Gurt.

I ask him to get dressed.

I pack their lunches in Ziploc bags. Each one gets a juice box,
a peanut butter sandwich (no jelly for this one, no crusts for that
one), Goldfish crackers, yogurt, and a note from me. Everything
in the lunch bag can be thrown away, which makes me not a

favorite among the environmentalists. But I read that the ancient Greeks were awarded not just for finishing the race but for finishing with their flame still burning. And I do think that tracking down lunchboxes daily might put my flame right out.

I write their names on the outside of each bag, and I doodle something fun and personal: Tucker gets a football or a soccer ball. Tyler lands a star or a paintbrush. After I finish doodling their names, I grab a piece of stationery and jot a note to Tyler's teacher. I begin, "Dear Mrs. C., I fear you may have some misinformation about my husband's death."

I ask Tyler to get dressed. He's halfway there, now wearing pants and a pajama shirt. "Lovey, put on a clean shirt, please."

"I like this one."

"But it's a pajama shirt." This is not enough of an argument, so I add, "And you've worn it to school twice already this week. Clean shirt, please."

"This is the fastest one I could find."

"I didn't ask you to find a fast one. I asked you to find a clean one." I point to the languishing laundry basket. He looks at me as if I'm pointing to a basket of gerbils. How could he possibly find the answer to the problem in the solution I have offered? I pluck a T-shirt from the top of the pile, one of his favorites with a big taco on the front and the words "I don't want to Taco 'bout it." With a great sigh of indignation, he takes off the pajama shirt and puts on the taco shirt, and then he turns on the TV as if he has met all the morning's demands.

"Tyler. Turn off the TV."

"What? I'm dressed!"

"Turn off the TV."

"What do you want from me? I did what you asked!"

We have had a version of this conversation every single morning of every school year. I stand firm in my stipulations regarding technology before school, and yet every morning he takes on the challenge to see if the rules still apply. I remind him of the caveats to the rule: Are you completely dressed? Shoes and socks? Is your homework finished and in your homework folder? Did you put your lunch in your backpack? And even if the answer to all the above is yes (which, I assure you, it couldn't be), then the final question: Were we on time to school yesterday? (I'm going out on a limb here and confidently saying we weren't. I consider it an epic victory when one more car follows me through the carpool lane. *Aha! We weren't the last ones today!*)

When I taught kindergarten, I could successfully take fifty-eight six-year-olds to the zoo, and yet I cannot effectively transition my two sons from the kitchen table to the car. It makes me crazy. The "out the door" alarm sounds on my phone, which happens to be an eerie sci-fi spaceship sound effect. We've also had the sounds of robots and ducks and train locomotives. The guys get to choose—just *please choose something, anything, that will motivate you to get out the door.*

And when it is time to go, one child is still in his pajamas, no shoes or socks on. I seriously pick him up and carry him to the car. I tell him to figure out a way to get dressed with his seat belt on. I grab his Crocs on my way out the door, which he protests because he has PE today and won't be able to participate since he doesn't have the right shoes on.

"Well, you had a whole hour, kiddo. A *whole hour* to find the right footwear. When the gym teacher asks today why you wore the wrong shoes, don't you *dare* tell him that your mom made you wear those, wouldn't find the right ones, or anything else that makes it sound like your irresponsibility is my fault!"

I want to enjoy these children. With all my heart, I want to.

When we arrive at the car, Tuck is a complete package of school readiness. (He does not get his penchant for preparedness from me.) Tyler is carrying his Ziploc lunch, his shoes, his "student of the week" poster, and his backpack, all while the hood of his jacket hangs from his head. (He gets these tendencies from me.)

I've thrown on a robe over jammies, and I'm banking on the hope that there will be absolutely no reason for me to get out of the car. This has sometimes failed me, and far too many people have seen me in this less-than state.

I really want to salvage some part of their morning with the happier version of me, so I converse as we back out of the driveway. "Anything special happening at school today, guys?"

"No. Nothing," says one boy.

"Probably not," says the other.

"Well, maybe the day will surprise you. Look for ways to be kind to others, okay? Remember that you're a leader."

"But I'm not the tallest," Tucker says. If only leadership were measured so simply.

"Well, please make sure you are the kindest."

We arrive at school at 8:38, which I consider to be a complete victory. The window of time for the drop-off is 8:25 to 8:40, so we are just under the wire. Tuck hops out at his first opportunity and makes a beeline for the door. I watch him blend into a sea of other kids, and I smile at the way he pats his buddies on the back and somehow walks exactly like his dad.

By the time Tyler gathers everything and goes inside, it's 8:42, and we are late again. I'm frustrated with our pattern, and yet there's something about the way his backpack hangs on his shoulders as he walks toward the school that is so heartbreakingly precious to me. What is it about that long walk that tugs on my heartstrings every blasted day? It's like a metaphor for all things parenting—helping him get out the door, preparing him in all the ways I feel that I can, watching him go, and then praying like everything that somehow he'll be safe until I see him again. I can't let myself drive away until I see him go inside. I let go of the tardiness and tell myself we'll try tomorrow—yet again—to be on time.

And now with two children safely at school, the day is mine. I go back home and get dressed for the day, complete with a scarf, bracelet, and lip gloss—always. Writers are a superstitious bunch, and we all have our lucky charms. Mine is lip gloss. I'll spend the day in my insulated world of words, stringing them together on the page or on the screen. I will not look at book sales or percentages or reviews because the numbers of it all can paralyze me faster than anything. I don't think about how many people are reading what I have to say or what they really think of it; I am learning to leave that off my plate of things to worry about. Writing is my job; parenting is my job. So I will love my boys, and I will write the next sentence. And the days will become years, and the words will become books, and the boys will become men.

At the end of their day, I meet them on the playground behind the school, and they run to me because they are still young enough to show their joy by running. We go to football practice or Tae Kwon Do, and I pay attention to the happenings of our life together, jotting some of them down to write about tomorrow.

I would love to tell you that we spend our evenings in some kind of structured routine of homework, dinner, baths, evening devotions, and bedtime stories. But we might have dinner at Chick-fil-A or perhaps spaghetti at home, we will collectively delay their homework responsibilities, baths will happen only if it's absolutely necessary, and we'll finish the day with bedtime TV in my bedroom.

They sleep on the floor in my room, which started as a privilege of spring break but then spread into what has become a nightly routine. Again, I wish I could tell you that the bedtime routine is filled with beautiful traditions and meaningful lessons. But the hard thing about bedtime is that it's at the end of the day, and by then I'm just d-o-n-e. Sometimes I do something silly and unexpected—like make up voices for their pajamas who are begging to be worn. Or I might sing a little ditty about boys and their dirty feet, but usually that only leads to wound-up boys, too much silliness that can no longer be stopped, a mom who is now miserable and snippy, and a lot of regret on my part as even with the best of intentions the day ends poorly.

So most often I stick with the routine conversation: we pray together, and we thank God for being bigger than anything we can think of. Tucker asks for good dreams "tonight and forever," and Tyler asks for no dreams at all, thank you very much. We say *amen,* and then one of them asks, "Mommy, who will take care of us if you die?"

"Grandma and Poppa."

"And what if they die?"

"Uncle Rob and Aunt Kate."

"And what if they die?"

My children were so small when they lost one parent in the span of a night's sleep. I want to assure them I will always be here in the morning, but that's an empty promise for sharp young minds that have been shattered. Instead, we talk through the worst. We follow that train of thought until we get to the end of the line and they can know there is a plan. Together we list the many, many people they know who would take care of them, and finally the plan is thick enough with safety that they can rest their minds.

We sleep with a lot of lights on in our house—night-light, closet light, hall light, bedside lamp—because fear of the dark is real and avoidable. Life is too short to be afraid, and a light bulb is a small price to pay when we all need the little boost to carry us through to morning. I sit on my bed and write in this gentle space of the evening. I like to imagine that the clicking sounds of my keyboard will be their lullaby, but they keep talking to me.

I used to make several trips down the hall every night to their bedrooms, habitually counting every one of the thirty-seven to thirty-nine steps from my bed to theirs. The sleeplessness was reminiscent of the newborn stage, except without the partner to commiserate with. I used to tell them they couldn't sleep in my room because this space would belong to me and the new dad; I also used to kiss them only on the cheek, telling them my lips were saved for the new dad. But here we are, four years later, and it's still just us, a very solid three with nobody else in sight. I'm tired of telling them no when I could just say yes. Childhood is too short to send them away or to save kisses for anybody else when together they make up my very kissable life. So for now I let them kiss me right on the lips. And for now I let them sleep on my floor. For now this works for us.

Each day requires a careful balance, a blend of this and that. A mix of TV and creative play, fast food and fresh fruits, firm boundaries and parental grace, routines and spontaneity, milk and juice, working inside and playing outside, play dates and stay-at-home days, trying new things and enjoying old favorites, encouraging boldness but keeping them safe, loving a free spirit but protecting the heart, learning to share and claiming a turn, teaching and learning, honoring nature and nurture, being gentle and firm, being able to say "I'm always here when you need me" and "But you don't always need me."

Some days feel a little lopsided. Mismatched socks and spilled milk and asking a son's forgiveness yet again—these are things I have learned from. Perfection isn't friendly or approachable, and since I desire most to be both friendly and approachable, well, then it's a great thing that I'm all things imperfect. The bottom line on this parenting thing is that I don't know how I'm doing this, and I had to relearn our stride. We needed to discover ourselves and who we are, and I needed to lead the cause in turning our world right side up. But I've found a rhythm and a balance that seems to be working well. At least for this season. At least for this day.

When I shut down the computer and decide to end the day, the credits roll through my mind with the scrolling list of things I didn't do right. In addition to the reckless limits on technology and nutrition, I have a male dog who is marking his territory in about fourteen places in my house, and he's doing his boy dog happy dance with anything that will stand still. Seriously, I can't get him neutered fast enough. And I dream of another land, far, far away, maybe even in a parallel universe, where it would not make a difference in my son's second-grade memories if I didn't make an appearance at his field trip tomorrow. At a farm. In the rain.

At some point I have to turn off my brain because here's what I've decided: I can't scrutinize myself over and over again. So I have a brief rubric, a few quick questions I ask myself: *Are they growing? Do they feel safe? Which of today's behaviors do I feel okay about apologizing for to his future wife?* Then I take inventory and I call it a day.

Parenting is a marathon, not a sprint, and one must measure it in decades, not days.

I snuggle under my covers, and I sleep in the middle of the bed since there's no reason to sleep on just one side when nobody is claiming the other side.

Good night, everybody in my house. Even if you're still awake, I'm going to sleep now.

three

There was a kidnapping in our neighborhood about six blocks from my home. The abductor was captured, the children are safe and home, and everyone's senses are heightened. I can't think much about that scene. Not really at all, actually. That's too close to home, in every sense of the word, in every sense of my world. News flash: suburbia does not mean safe.

The profilers on the case determined that this abductor had been looking for a chance to take a child—or in the case of this kidnapping, two children. I told the boys what happened. They have to know; they have to be safe; they have to be smart. They've *got* to be. Tyler suggested we put inside him an ink device that would explode all over him and the kidnapper if my child is too far from me. That way, he tells me, everyone could know at a moment's notice that he's not safe, he's not with a safe person, and he needs help—fast. Sort of like the devices to prevent shoplifting in clothing stores. Other than a few logistical hiccups, his idea is pure brilliance. I'm not above it.

God, keep them safe. Please, Jesus. Keep them safe.

After Robb died, a mentor in my life told me, "Tricia, here's what you need to know: studies have shown that children who have lost a parent need only one thing—*one thing*! They need the unconditional love of one adult in their lives."

Just one? Well, I can be that one, and in addition to me, my kids have many people in their lives who love, love, love them. There's nothing they could do to not be my kids anymore. So all I have to do is love them? Well, I can do that.

It was pretty rosy in my mind at first. I didn't really recognize the ramifications of the word *unconditional*. The call was not just to love them but to love them always, consistently, and without condition. To commit to this life with them, even when none of the three of us wanted to do this together anymore. To love them when they were less charming than they had been as newborns. To stick with them. To ride the highs and lows so that they knew—no matter what happened and no matter how hard they might have tried otherwise—I would never stop loving them.

One thing I think is important to realize in tandem with the word *unconditional* is that love is a decision. Love is clean clothes to wear to school. Love is clean underwear. Love is signed permission slips. Love is groceries in the cupboard. Love is routines and predictability.

When my heart has been too weak to overflow with crazy amounts of affection, I could remind myself that my children were healthy and happy and that they had their mom. And there was nothing they could do to change any of those facts.

I think I feel most overwhelmed with single parenting when I am worried for my children. I sit at this coffee shop, and I cry over their hearts, their learning, their impulses, their grief, and their needs. There is nobody to say it to, nobody who will carry this quite as deeply as I do, though a few come very close. I am their only parent.

And then I am reminded that I am not their only parent. Their Creator knows their hearts. Their Counselor knows their worries. Their Father holds them close. I am their mom. And I am not alone.

I read this verse tucked in the middle of a psalm: "You did not forget to punish the guilty or listen to the cries of those in need" (Psalm 9:12).

You did not forget. Those first four words capture my heart, prompting me to make a list of the things my God has not forgotten. Sure, I could list them in bulleted sentence fragments with just a few words to highlight each one. But each one matters to me—and to him. So I write each thought as a sentence, since each one is a complete truth.

You did not forget about me.

You did not forget about Tucker.

You did not forget about Tyler.

You did not forget about my aching heart.

You did not forget that my children are fatherless.

You did not forget how I love to love.

You did not forget that I am single

or, even more so, that I am a single mom.

You did not forget that children everywhere are hungry.

You did not forget about the senseless violence that is happening everywhere.

You did not forget that you are the Lord of lords, the Prince of Peace.

You did not forget that we need you.

You did not forget to be faithful.

You did not forget that we are waiting for you.

You did not forget your promises.

You did not forget to remember.

You did not forget the sparrows.

Even as I wait, he has not forgotten.

I had to learn to stop telling myself "I can't do this." When I have been particularly overwhelmed, that has been the voice I heard in my head and even the words I said out loud to myself.

When I was in college, I learned about the phenomenon that psychologists call the "self-fulfilling prophecy." Negative thoughts produce negative actions, which eventually produce negative results. So if I told myself I surely couldn't do this, then it was highly likely that, indeed, I wouldn't be able to finish the day. Let alone the marathon of parenting.

Let's take a moment here. If a "friend" in my life told me repeatedly that I couldn't do this job, that I don't have what it takes, I would most assuredly stop spending time with that person. But I can't get away from myself. Nowhere to go. So I had to teach myself to speak differently to myself, to "love one another as myself" or to love myself as I would love another person. I would never say those things to a friend, so why did I let myself look in the mirror and tear myself down? Every time I beat up myself, I was helping the Enemy. He's pretty effective at defeating me on his own; I intend to give him no help.

I don't remember it very clearly, but many people have told me that in between my waves of shock and silence on the day that Robb died, I fiercely said out loud, "I will do this. I will not be taken down. I will raise these children, and I will do this!"

I barely remember saying those words, and I certainly lost hold of them in the weeks, months, and years to follow. But at the very start, I said those words. Perhaps it was a promise I chose to make in front of all those witnesses.

I.

Will.

Do.

This.

Part Two

in our family

My son comes home from school with a fair and genuine question. "Mommy, a boy in my class has two moms and no dad. How does that work?" Oh, the complexities of the answer.

He drops the iPod and shouts, "Oh, $#&@! Wait . . . Mommy, are we allowed to say $#&@?"

He practices trash-talking in a game of street hockey in the neighborhood. "What's your name? Shut up! *It doesn't matter what your name is!*" "But, Mom, the World Wide Wrestlers say that."

He sees a magazine picture of a woman in her scant bathing suit at the checkout in the grocery store. "Dude. That chick is so hot. What, Mom? Why can't I say that?"

These things pop up all the time, newly acquired behaviors and habits followed shortly by the question "Why can't I? My friends do it." What do you do when your child begins to question you and your decisions? Or more powerful yet, how do you resist the sponge effect of peer pressure when your child begins to adopt traits and habits from a family with very different values? How do you solve the ever-present, age-old dilemma of "If your friends jumped off a cliff, would you?"

I have adopted three words that are my standard go-to: "in our family." In our family, there are some ground rules that are true—always—for us. My children may find other things to be true when they enter the homes of their friends or the communities they're involved in at church or on sports teams, but the identity of our family is solid. "In our family" this is what we do.

My guys love to give a name to whatever the three of us are doing together, and they call us That Family. We have been The Hot Dog Eating Family. The Gutter Ball Bowling Family. The Sing in the Car Family. The Friday Night Pizza and a Movie Family. The Frownie Face Family. The Chocolate Milk Mustache Family. The Flip-Flop Family. Or after a long day in the park wearing those flip-flops, we are the Dirty Feet Family. I think everyone is born with a need to belong, and the greatest sense of belonging should happen within a family. When we have these silly and random moments all doing the same ridiculous thing, we claim it as one of the threads that holds us together. The great thing about these silly examples is that it has given the boys a sense of identity, a sense of who we are. I aim to lay this foundation when there's no tension in the air so that later, when they're mad at me and pushing the boundaries of who they can be and who they will become, I can go back to that core truth of what is true *in our family.*

I can answer the questions like the ones above within the context of what is true in our family.

"Families look different, and they come in all shapes and sizes. But in our family, the children have one mom and one dad."

"In our family, we use words that are smart and intentional, and that rude word is thoughtless. It doesn't show how smart and thoughtful you are."

"In our family, you can absolutely be confident in what you

do and who you are. But you can never imply that someone doesn't matter just because he's on a different team."

"In our family, we don't use the names of farm animals to talk about girls. Chick, fox, cow, dog—I don't care what you mean by it. Women are not synonymous with animals."

I've watched them apply this filter for making their choices as they are learning there are certain decisions we make and priorities we set in our family. This has helped them see, unequivocally, that *we are a family*, even though Robb has died. We are a family and we are whole. And we know who we are.

"Mommy, who is your husband?"

"Daddy is."

Or, wait. Daddy was. Is? Was? Those verb tenses get me every time.

"Actually, I don't have a husband anymore. But when Daddy was alive, he was my husband."

Yes, love conquers the grave. But on a questionnaire when it asks, "Are you married or single?" I'm single. He was my husband.

"Do you think Poppa could be your husband, Mommy?"

"No, he's my dad."

"Do you think I could be your husband?"

"No, kiddo. It just doesn't work that way." *It's okay, buddy. Not every mommy has a husband.*

I remember registering Tucker for kindergarten in those first weeks after Robb died. The questionnaire asked, "Does your child live in a single-parent home?" Now, I know from my years as a teacher that this question is a practical one, not a voice of judgment. They just need to know if the child receives mail at more than one address. They need to know how many phone numbers to list and who might answer at each number. Still, I struggled with how to answer this question.

Single-parent home? Yes.

Divorced home? No.

Broken home? No.

If I may be so bold, I'd like to tackle a misconception about single parenting. Far too many people refer to single-parent families as "broken homes." To those hung up and insistent on using this phrase, may I advise, "We don't all consider ourselves broken. Many of us feel that through God's help and a great deal of personal effort, our homes have been healed. Even if—as with my guys and me—the healing didn't come overnight." The phrase "single-parent home" has so many implications to which I was unwilling to acquiesce. And yet my choices were two boxes: yes or no.

So do you know what I did? I crossed out the yes *and* the no. I wrote in black, bold, daring letters: WIDOW. That word answered so many questions all at one time, and it's all I truly needed to offer.

Single moms are moms. And that is valiant, courageous, constant work. I read somewhere this saying about single moms that I love: no matter how we came on board, we are in the same boat.

Divorced women, I have a quick word for you lovely warriors:

you especially have my sympathy. When my husband died, I floated in a sea of support. People provided food—many lasagnas and casseroles—childcare, money, friendship, and sympathy. But shortly after my loss, I walked alongside one of my best girl-friends as her husband left her, she filed for divorce, her home was foreclosed, she enrolled her four children in new schools, and she began working multiple jobs in order to independently meet the needs of her family. Other friends and I loved her and did every-thing we could to support her. But she didn't have the tragic story that compelled people to respond. Nonetheless, she was a single mom who, quite frankly, had lost far more than I had.

My husband died; her husband chose to leave. Yes, grief from death is a deep cut, but it's a clean cut. The grief from divorce is deep and jagged. It's a wound I do not know, and my heart aches if you are one who must carry your children through this field of land mines.

In my observation, when people talk to a very young girl, they kneel down to her level, make eye contact, and ask gentle ques-tions. And in my experience, when they want to talk to a young boy, they start with ruffling his hair, tackling, tickling, punching him on the arm, or wrestling.

Here's the thing. As much as I can (and God knows I try— *God knows I try*), I get that this physical roughhousing thing is what boys do, what they need. And I allow room in my life and in my heart for the insanity of the pace of my boys. But I'm trying with my whole self to teach my guys to be gentlemen too. Or to be self-controlled. Or to be civilized. Or maybe not to act like gorillas.

So when some well-meaning person comes up and tackles my boy in the lobby after church, wrestles him to the ground, and tickles him until he's giggling for air, it's not my favorite thing. While I get the sentiment and appreciate the effort to engage my son, in a moment that person is going to walk away and get on with his day, and I will have a laughing, coughing, Tasmanian-wrestling, wound-up-Energizer-Bunny, please-God-help-me child who now feels that he was right all along, that this kind of behavior actually is acceptable, despite what his ridiculous, unknowing mother tells him.

So how about we give this a try: *shake his hand.* He's been working on the firm grip of a young man, and you can give him another chance to practice. Make eye contact. Show him that a man looks people in the eye with dignity. Ask him a question. Expect him to answer; I certainly expect him to answer! And show him that a great way to earn the attention and respect of other people is to engage them in appropriate conversation.

Not so much with the tackling and wrestling. They can save that for the football field and the playground. Or the kitchen table. (We're working on that too.)

five

The start of a new soccer season always reminds me of the first year we ventured into the subculture of suburban soccer. Tucker was five, Tyler was three, and it was generally a bad experiment. Preschool soccer teams look a whole lot like a litter of puppies toppling over one another to be the first one out of the cardboard box.

On the field Tyler dotted his forehead with sideline chalk—his own version of Ash Wednesday. He commando-crawled across the field—a sneak attack, if you will. He lifted his shirt to show off the remains of the monster-truck tattoo on his tummy. He took his own approach to defending the goal: he stood on the other side of the goal, poking his face through the net, roaring at the other team. He found treasures on the ground, like beer bottle caps or a pink plastic butterfly ring. Oh, the things one can find as he commando-crawls during a soccer game.

He negotiated with Coach Sarah: "I'll run if you will." Except she's the coach, and it's not her job to run. He told her she was being a bully. She said graciously, "Yes, I am. Now come over here and get in the game." She's a girl after my own heart. I encouraged Coach Sarah to start writing a blog titled "I Coach Preschool Soccer." She'd have no shortage of amusing content.

Meanwhile, Tuck perfected this wide-girth strategy, running around the perimeter of the clump of other children chasing the soccer ball. He had his eye on the ball and his head in the game, but he was taking this weird passive approach. He seemed to be anticipating the trajectory of the ball, waiting for it to come to him when somebody gave it a good kick. It's actually a fairly reasonable approach, except that on the preschool team, they don't play with goalkeepers or allow blocking. So his team didn't really benefit from his strategy since he scored no goals.

Somehow this made me inordinately frustrated, as if I'm any kind of athlete. I heard myself shouting, "Tuck! Get in there, buddy! Go! Why are you way out there? What are you doing?" That's right. I became *that mom*. The competitive one on the sidelines. I had no intention of becoming *that mom,* and I barely recognized myself.

I, their very unathletic and non-soccer-playing mom, gave them off-the-field tips. "Hey, Tuck? It's not selfish or rude to get in there and get the ball. I realize it's counterintuitive after the things we do at home, but, kiddo, *go after that ball.*"

"Hey, Tyler? Engage, kiddo. Just engage."

At the end of one game, Tyler was awarded the sticker for best sportsmanship since that day he was better at cheering than playing. Another week he received the sticker for best defense since he knew what the word meant. That's what it came down to. Can anyone verbally identify the term? Aha! Sticker for you! We'll work on application and execution another time.

Tucker most often won the sticker for best defense because

he got close to the ball a couple of times, and among the litter of tumbling puppies, that counted for something.

The following spring, with a year of life and skills behind him, Tuck was ready to play another season. When I asked Tyler if he wanted to be on the team, he said, "Why? I already did that." He thought Tuck's return to soccer was similar to repeating a year of kindergarten; in his mind it must be remedial.

This year—our third season—the sport of soccer has a very sweet and precious joy for our family. Tuck has become this powerhouse kicker; he can kick the ball the entire length of the field, sometimes straight into the goal. What he may lack in accuracy is more than compensated by strength. In fact his coach teases that Tucker's leg is an additional player on the team, one deserving respect and maybe even its own number. Every time Tucker kicks another goal, the crowd roars, shouting and ringing cowbells. And the spirit I see in Tucker's eyes shows me that he has found the joy of the game and the intoxication of the audience. With each kick I know that we have just bought another season.

As for Tyler, after taking a year off with disinterest, he decided to join the team again. Though I never thought I'd say it when we started this sport three years ago, he engaged the game by his own choice and became one of the team's best defenders. He gave it a try, and he knows that he *can,* which is very different from *wanting to.* Given his choice, he'll choose glue and paints and markers over any ball you offer. So he and I are exploring his other options, looking to find his very favorite niche. He would very much like to take tap-dancing classes, so I'm in search of a dance studio that offers more than pink tutus and the tap-ballet combination.

The thing is, I hear all the warnings against overscheduling kids. And I agree; there are so many options and invitations every day of the week, and we could run ourselves ragged with a tight calendar. I don't want to exhaust my boys with extracurricular craziness. But if you could see the way Tucker's eyes light up on the field, you'd know it's part of who he is. Eliminate this after-school plan, and I really think part of him might fade a shade or two. Competition runs in his veins, and sports are his way of thinking. He comes alive when he's part of a team, and this sacred thread holds the rest of the seams in his life together.

And if you're a second born—or further down the line in your family—then you know there is some subtle scorekeeping going on that will follow Tyler the rest of his life, especially if I don't explicitly demonstrate my love for his skills and interests as well. Although Tyler's interests aren't as widely cheered as Tucker's, and while I don't receive daily fliers and handouts and invitations for the artist's activities, he's an artist, and this is his way. His eyes light up and his spirit soars when he is creating. So I look for the activities that are his, and I add them to the calendar.

The world cheers more loudly for the football team, but the world needs art and music and dance and laughter. In my two boys I have an athlete and an artist. I am learning to lean into their differences; it's the key to "living to tell about it."

six

There are some sounds I've learned to tune out in nearly a decade of parenting, but the shattering of glass will get my attention every time.

It was almost bedtime, and Tucker was warming up a rice heating pad that helps his stomach settle at the end of the day. When he pulled it out of the microwave, it stuck to some Easy Mac that had spilled during the dinner hour. The glass plate in the microwave—the one that is thick and strong and designed to withstand just about anything—came out with the rice pack, crashed to the floor, and shattered into wicked pieces and shards of every size, one such piece cutting deeply into Tucker's shin and his big toe.

I was running to him before the glass could settle on the floor. I was calling out, "It's okay! It's okay, buddy!" I suspect I was talking to all three of us even before I approached the situation. At the same time, he was running to me, shouting, "I've got blood! I've got blood!" We met in the stairwell, and that's where we stayed until the paramedics arrived. I surprised myself with my calm voice, my knowledge of what to do, and my courage that owned the room and took charge of the situation. It's amazing what you can do when you have to.

Tyler, one of the epic heroes of the story, called my parents.

"Grandma! Come fast! Right now! Tucker is bleeding and it's so bad and just come right now!" "Poppa! Come! Come quick! Oh, you're with Grandma? Then bring her!"

And he dialed 911 and held the speakerphone next to my face so I could talk to the dispatcher. I'm pretty leery about calling 911. It's not my favorite thing to do, and I will explore any other avenue before I have to call in the big guns. But when you're holding your son's leg together, applying pressure and catching blood on your arms and pajamas, it might be time to call for reinforcements. I knew I couldn't get him anywhere until the bleeding stopped, and I knew I couldn't stop the bleeding.

There were two positive outcomes from the phone call, in addition to the quick response and medical assistance. When I had called 911 before, my husband was dying on my bedroom floor. That time, as the dispatcher asked me each question to gauge the severity of the situation, my every answer was frantic and hopeless: *No, he's not conscious. No, he's not breathing. No, I can't find his pulse. Please, just help me. Please fix him. Please.*

This time the phone call was calming to me as I realized with every answer that this situation was manageable and controlled. *Yes, he is conscious. Yes, he is making eye contact. Yes, he can answer me. Yes, I do believe I can hang up the phone and wait for them to get here.*

And as a cherry on top of the sundae of optimism, my sons listened to my phone call on the speakerphone, and all the wonder and fear of calling 911 was demystified. Should they ever need to call (*Please, God, not anytime soon*), they know what the voices sound like, what questions they ask, how to stay calm, and what to do next.

Within minutes my home was filled with firemen and paramedics. (I seriously am pretty sure "handsome" is in the job description.) I stayed on the stairs, holding Tucker's leg together, until the handsome men replaced my hands and towels with their own. They talked to him and to me, distracting us under the guise of making small talk.

"Look at this, buddy! What happened here?"

Tuck told the story for the first time, which began in his linear mind with the question "Well, do you know what a rice compress is?" I wanted to teach him a quicker, more efficient way to say, "A plate fell out of the microwave and tore into my leg," but it wasn't my story to tell, and my interruptions wouldn't have helped anyone—least of all my son. The firemen and paramedics listened to his retelling, and they lightened the room with playful bets with one another on how many stitches Tuck would need.

With Tucker bound together we chose not to ride in the ambulance to the hospital. As one handsome man told me, "Ma'am, we can take him, but we can't use lights and sirens, so you won't get there any faster. And we won't treat the wound, so really all we would do is send you a bill in a few days."

I appreciated his honesty. And his chestnut eyes.

They carried Tuck to the backseat of the car and buckled him in. "Well, Tuck, come by the fire station on Tuesday or Wednesday of next week. We'll be there, and we would like to hear the full report. Deal?"

Deal. We waved them on their way to save other people from their emergencies. Just before I got in the car with my dad, Tyler came running out of the house, crying my name. "Mommy, I'm not brave anymore. I'm not brave."

I knelt on the sidewalk and hugged him. "You are very brave."

"But I'm crying."

"Oh, sweet boy. Being brave doesn't mean you don't ever cry. It means you did what you had to do. And you were one of the heroes tonight."

His adrenaline had just run out, he realized what was happening, and despite my mother being with him, he wasn't leaving my side or his brother's. So we made it a family affair. Tyler climbed into the backseat with me, my mom followed in her car, and all five of us were off to the hospital at record speed.

In the process of our recurring trips to the ER, I have learned how to advocate like nobody's business. "This is my son, these are his daily medications, these are his allergies, and he is tolerant—or resistant, if you'd rather—to lidocaine. It doesn't work. Nothing in the -caine family works on my son, and this is not the day when we will experiment with other drugs to see what works. He will need to be asleep when you fix him, please."

They looked at me with eyes that questioned how this could possibly be true. "Tell me more about this. What experiences have you had with lidocaine? Are you sure it doesn't work?" Scenes flashed before my eyes. My son in excruciating pain while a nurse suggested he was just nervous. A doctor suggesting we just do the stitches and get it over with since there didn't seem to be anything more they could give him for the pain. The maxillofacial specialist who taught me there are times when a kid just needs to sleep through the whole thing.

So I repeated the above, as often as needed. I was a formidable force of maternal adrenaline, and I would settle for nothing less than conscious sedation. Seriously. Warrior Mama.

There was much discussion over whether he could be treated at this children's hospital or if he would need to be transferred to the main campus. In the end we settled into their procedure room, a dollhouse version of an operating room, and the anesthetist put Tucker into a twilight state that carried his mind away to a blissful place he will never remember.

The doctor said to me, "I need you to please be seated because this is usually when parents pass out." And that was my cue to step out of this scene. I stopped at the family nutrition center and grabbed a Popsicle for Tyler, and I went to sit in the waiting room with my mom and my little guy.

My dad stayed next to Tucker for the whole procedure, and he confirmed that I had made the right decision to slip out the door. The twilight medication did not keep Tucker from feeling the pain, but it would keep him from remembering it later, and they tell me memory is the worst part of pain. His sedated but conscious self groaned and cried as they stitched him together. He started talking to them about "having three ears," so they gave him additional meds to put him further under. He resisted every stitch they put in, so instead of doing twenty small stitches, they gave him six big ones. A wounded leg doesn't need the kind of cosmetic attention that a face does, and we all know that a bold scar paves the way for a good story to tell a girl someday. So they

sewed the wound closed enough, and they told me to expect scar-
ring and "seepage." (I have now added that to the list of words I
won't be saying.)

We all got back home by about one o'clock in the morning,
and I settled my crew on the couch for a family slumber party
while my parents took care of the crime scene of broken glass in
the kitchen.

There aren't enough words in the world to describe how
thankful I am for my parents. There just aren't. Before she left, my
mom kissed my cheek. She said, "That boy of yours has put you
through more than you and your brother together ever did to me.
And he's not even nine years old." She suggested I keep a journal
to log all his scars, injuries, stitches, and head wounds. I started
one when he was small, but injuries kept coming, and now I am
so far behind that it overwhelms me to try to catch up with all the
documentation. In the meantime I've decided to join Aflac Insurance since they reimburse in cash every time we go to the ER, and
I'm figuring that could be some supplemental, part-time income
for the next ten years.

The saddest of the sad was that Tucker would be on the injured list for the first few games of his football season, which
started that weekend. I assure you my son waits all year long for
these ten weeks. The good news is that the doctor approved his
going to the Broncos game the next day. Some friends had given
us their tickets, a gracious and unexpected gift that ultimately
crossed a major event off Tuck's bucket list. Attending a pro-
football game was one of his life's greatest hopes, let alone the

glory of seeing his favorite team. I was pretty much ready to strap him to my back and carry him to the stadium if he wasn't allowed to walk on his own, so when the doc gave his approval, he managed to partly assuage the heartbreak of Tucker's own football season.

"Here's a hard-soled shoe, kid. Enjoy the game."

In the exhaustion of the next few days, I made one small mistake after another. When you have enough parts of the day that are just a little bit not right, then the day can begin to feel like a whole lot of wrong.

I had forgotten to order Spirit Wear T-shirts, and the deadline had now passed me by. I had sent the money to school, just not in time to order the shirts. I needed to track down the PTA mom who handles all things involving the pride of our school colors so my children wouldn't be the disgrace of their classrooms on the first Friday of each month when there's a grade-level competition to see which class displays the most school spirit. Surely I could not allow my children to be the reason the fifth graders would win or, worse yet, the reason the second and third graders would lose.

I had gotten a call from the school's health assistant because it seems I had turned in an unmarked inhaler for Tucker. I didn't include his name on it, or doctor's orders, or an official pharmacy label. For all they knew, I could have found that little puffing device in the gutter next to the mall. They made a strong point . . .

medications should have a few more requirements. I meant well by making sure my son's breathing meds would be close by if he needed them, but I hadn't made it possible for anyone to actually administer the medications.

I had delivered the boys to the school for each of their appointments for beginning-of-the-year assessments, but I hadn't read the fine print. We waited in the library for their turns but later discovered that was where parents were supposed to wait during the testing. I was supposed to deliver each child to his classroom for his individual appointment. We were in the library as their time slots came and went, in the wrong place at the right time.

Tucker was still in bandages from his falling-out with the microwave plate, and the bandage on his toe had started to slip at school. He went to the nurse to ask for assistance. She let me know later that she *had* helped him and also that his feet were terribly smelly. Well, yes. This did not surprise me. A boy who is almost nine years old has the feet of a young man. I had done my best to keep his wound dry while it was healing, but in keeping him out of the bathtub, I had not accounted for the stench of sweat and the risk of the school nurse having to unwrap it all. I meant well.

I had forgotten to mail the check to the lawn guy. I wrote the check, but I didn't drop the envelope in the mail.

Tyler had Tae Kwon Do after school; I had washed his uniform, but a stray black sock had joined the ranks of the whites in the washing machine, turning far too many things into a dull gray. When he put on his uniform for class, he looked like he represented the dingy whites of the off-brand detergent in a Tide commercial.

I'm telling you—I was consistently almost right but just enough off to be wrong.

Tyler and I were both a little unsettled to see a substitute instructor in the Tae Kwon Do studio. Instead of the normal master, Matt, we met Master Tim, who was tall, lanky, pimply, barely out of high school, and probably fresh from his afternoon shift at McDonald's. Not that I have a problem with any of these things, but Matt *is* a professional black-belt master of Tae Kwon Do, he runs a tight classroom, and his expectations are high but clear and reasonable. I had gotten used to his methods in a sport I knew so very little about.

My first indication that things were not going to go the way of Master Matt was the prolonged warmup session that, frankly, seemed to indicate Master Tim's delight in his own power. He had the children running laps—running, running, running—while he stood and watched smugly. Now, Tyler had recently won the award in second grade for running the most laps in one stretch (ninety-six!), so he wasn't fazed by this warmup routine. Still, I watched closely. The children asked for water; Master Tim told them to keep running. I had a bad feeling in my spirit, and I'm pretty sure I showed my suspicion with telltale narrowed eyes and furrowed brow.

In the poetic color representation of Tae Kwon Do, Tyler wore a white belt, which means "innocence." He had been taking the class for only a few weeks. Master Tim paired him against a student who wore a red belt, which means "danger." The red belt is just below the famed expertise of the black belt, and a student with the skills of a red belt can be very dangerous if he has not yet learned self-control. Add to that, this kid was a good forty pounds bigger than my seven-year-old. Master Tim didn't require the older, bigger, more skilled boy to wear the pads the other children wear for sparring. To this day I do not know why. But he put him against my child, and he said, "I want to see two minutes of punching and kicking."

Tyler was fiercely brave in the face of this giant. He stayed on the mat and in the fight, blocking and defending as well as he had learned. But he was no match against a kid armed with red-belt skills and no self-control. I sensed Tyler's fear in the nonverbal ways that only a son's mother knows.

Two things happened simultaneously to set me in motion:

1. Tyler cast a split-second side glance at me. Out of the corner of his eye, he gave me a quick flash of eye contact to see if I was watching, if I saw what was happening to him, if I was ready to help him. I wouldn't embarrass my child by getting involved and fighting a battle he could handle on his own, but that side glance was all I needed.

2. The kid with the red belt said to Tyler, "Come on and fight me, you big baby."

That was *it*. Let me tell you, I am not often the irate Mama Bear, but when I am, look out. I called Tyler's name, usurping Master Tim's authority. I dismissed him from the fight, and his bottled tears started to spill as he came running to me.

I began untying Tyler's pads as my eyes met Master Tim's, and I said, "We are going to stop now."

I snapped my fingers to get Tucker's attention, a method I am opposed to but felt completely reduced to. Tuck was enraptured in some game of yellow minions on the iPad, and he had been oblivious to the whole scene, which was probably a good thing since he professed later that he would have kicked Red Belt in the hip if he had seen it happen. "Tuck," I snapped, "gather your things. We are leaving."

I swear to you, the laces of those pads were tied in sailor's knots. I was sweating, my son was crying, and I could not get those knots untied fast enough.

"Sorry, white-belt kid," the bully said to my son.

I looked at him as the last knot finally released in my hands. I loosened the laces behind Tyler's back, and I said, "His name is Tyler."

Master Tim spoke but a little too late. "Hesed, you have to show self-control. That boy only has a white belt."

Now he speaks? And he calls my son *that boy*?

"His name is *Tyler*." I spat my words at him. With the fierce stride of a scorned mother, I walked out of the studio with my young son's hand in mine and my older son trailing, wide eyed. When we stepped into the hallway, I wrapped my arms around Tyler. I could feel his rib cage racking with silent sobs.

"Nobody will ever, ever do that to you. That is not okay, and I will never allow it! Do you understand me? *Do you understand me?*" And that's when I realized I had displaced my anger; I was using the angry tone I felt toward Master Tim in the words I needed to comfort my child. Sometimes a child doesn't need his mom to speak. He just needs her heartbeat. So I held my son next to my racing heart and breathed deeply, waiting for it to slow down. As he unwound, I think all his adrenaline flowed into me by osmosis. I was so spun up. I felt as if I could run a marathon, as if maybe I *should* run a marathon—even though I don't run at all anymore—just to channel this fury. But there was no time for that; there was nothing to kick and nobody to punch. There was only my sons and this moment.

We walked to the car while I assured them, with a kinder tone, that I would never allow that to happen again. I told them I would begin making phone calls (and I did) until people in authority listened to me (and they did) and I could be sure that instructor was fired (and he was).

When we got home, I gave them access to enough technology to equip a library in a small country: iPhone, iPod, iPad, Mac, and, as a backup, fifty-seven DVR recordings of iCarly and, of course, Netflix as needed. I climbed the stairs to my bedroom and locked the door. I went into my closet and closed the door. Behind the sound barrier of two rooms and a stairwell, I fell to the floor and cried harder than I had in at least a year.

I cried because I didn't have Robb, and that made me feel as though I didn't have anyone. I cried because I so badly wanted him to hold me, to lift my chin so my eyes met his, to say, "It's okay, baby girl. I've got this."

I shouted at God. "You said you would be near to me! You said you are near to the brokenhearted and you are close to the crushed in spirit. You said that, and where are you? You said you are the Father to the fatherless, and don't you see that my children only have a mom? I can't find you, and I don't know where you are, and I feel as if you're not keeping your promises to me. And I'm so angry with you. And I'm so angry. I'm. So. Angry."

I shook my fists in the air, then pounded them into the carpet. I grabbed a T-shirt from my dirty-clothes pile, I stuffed it into my mouth, and I screamed against the balled-up cotton. I cried until I had surrendered to the magnitude of it all, and I lay in a heap on the closet floor, comforting myself and stroking my own hair. I begged God for his presence, and I felt nothing. I cried because nobody was sharing my anger. I cried because it was too much anger for one person to carry.

I opened the closet door and stepped into my bathroom. I ran cold water on a washcloth and held it to my swollen eyes and my throbbing forehead. The bottle of Excedrin rattled in my trembling hand as I poured two pills into my hand. I heard them against my teeth as I put the pills in my mouth, and I gulped water from the filmy glass I use when I brush my teeth. I slammed the cup down on the counter. I leaned close to my reflection in the mirror, and I looked into the face of an aged, tired woman.

I don't know how much time passed, but eventually I came downstairs. I found my children just as I had left them: their eyes glued to screens. They glanced in my direction. "Hey, Mommy. What are we having for dinner?"

I stood over the kitchen sink and opened the dishwasher with one hand. I loaded dirty glasses into the top rack and answered them with an even, steady voice that sounded almost normal. "If you'll bring me my phone, I'll order a pizza."

seven

S omehow, September sneaks up on me. Tuck has been turning a year older in the first week of September for many years now, and yet every year we finish summer, they go back to school, we're getting into our routine, and—*wham!*—it's suddenly the day before my son's birthday, and I have to get my act together with some memorable treat for all his classmates. For the record, I have never forgotten his birthday. But it just always sneaks up on me in its sneaky September way.

So it was the night before cupcake day for my birthday boy. This year his birthday was on Saturday, and we needed eighteen cupcakes for the collective total of students and teachers in his class on Friday. We were out of time for the fresh-baked variety, so I asked my mom to pick up two dozen at the area megastore.

She called. "Trish? Do you have muffin tins?"

"I do."

"Let's make cupcakes instead. The ones on display are fifteen dollars for a dozen, and they're hideously ugly. You would want to drop them off without your name on them. I'm not kidding. You can't do that." She knows me well.

The contagious joy of my little bakers quickly took over. They had big dreams and big plans with a strong emphasis on blue frosting and sprinkles. Before we could begin, though, they confessed a flushing incident earlier in the day. The Captain

America underpants were lost somewhere in the pipes. Tyler burst into tears over his beloved superhero, very clearly gone. I mean, gone. I was near tears too because, quite frankly, I haven't the first idea about plumbing, and I had no idea what the repercussions might be.

Meanwhile Tucker called from another bathroom, "Hey, Mommy? I have a problem in here!" Turns out, in the midst of the blockage at one end of the hallway, another toilet became clogged elsewhere in the house. *Seriously? I need this?* I became a plunging wild woman. I ran from bathroom to bathroom, plunging with all my might.

The boys trailed back and forth after me. "Mommy? Did the water go down? Did the water go down? Can we make cupcakes yet? How about now? Can I have some frosting? How about now?" *Oh, for crying out loud!* Things went down. All of it. I'll spare you the details except to say that I wasn't exactly ecologically friendly. I just kept flushing. Keep the water moving, folks. No time for things to stop and settle in.

And finally, the moment we had all been waiting for: let's make some cupcakes. We made them from a mix because I know my high-altitude limits. We opted for homemade frosting because it's so easy and so delicious . . . unless one realizes too late that she is nearly out of powdered sugar. *Oh, right. That.* And officially out of blue food coloring. *Oh, right. That too.*

A quick and frantic perusal of the pantry delivered one canister of Pillsbury cream-cheese frosting (which I may or may not have been saving for a night of desperation, when I may or may not have devoured it in one sitting with a spoon). A strong soapbox of persuasion convinced Tucker to change his color choice, and we went with green. *Whew. Carry on.*

I'm not going so far as to say that baked goods are a point of pride for me, but I will say that I can be kind of a stickler for a pleasing presentation. If I choose not to buy, then I want it to be clear why I chose to make them instead. I need pretty. (I just do. Don't judge me.) In the most inopportune moment, my Pampered Chef Easy Accent Decorator let me down. A small hairline fracture in the little doo-dah ring led to mass destruction. No joke. I have texture issues, and I can't handle sticky anything on my fingers. *Cannot handle.*

I was squeezing pretty ribbons of frosting onto the cupcakes, all while minty-green goo poured out from another crevasse faster than I could keep up. Frosting. Everywhere. I was shrieking, trying to catch it all while little boys were sneaking finger licks.

"Hey! Stop licking! Go wash your hands. Did you put the spoon in your mouth? Then it's dirty now, Tuck. Get a new one. Hey! No fingers in the frosting. Hey! *Hey!* Wash your hands. Tyler, the spoon is in your hair. Get a new one. *Hey! What did I say?*"

My mom, ever the voice of wisdom, said, "Perhaps we could just frost these with a knife? The old-fashioned way?"

What? Are you kidding me? Absolutely not. I would not be defeated. *Pretty ribbons of frosting, you will submit to my authority in your life.* I kept frosting cupcakes, counting them one by one. "Please, do we have eighteen yet? We just need eighteen. For the love of all things frosted, do we have eighteen?"

We had sixteen presentable cupcakes. I whipped out two

more blessed little green lovelies, complete with sprinkles. Done. We hid the ugly ones. I tucked them into the center of the middle tier of the cupcake tree (I told you I have high aspirations), leaning heavily on the benefit of people's assumptions that cupcakes get damaged on their way to school and that surely Tricia didn't frost them this way and send them in this condition.

Just then Tyler said, "Hey, Mommy? My water won't go down to the ocean."

Um, what? Turns out he had run to the bathroom in between sprinkles, and the toilet wouldn't flush. Again with the mad-woman plunging.

I went to Krispy Kreme to pick up doughnuts for the birthday breakfast, since we surely couldn't eat the cupcakes that were re-served for the classmates. But Krispy Kreme had a sign on the door that said, "A key component in our machinery has broken, keeping us from making our delicious doughnuts today. We apol-ogize for the inconvenience."

I stood there and thought, *Well, I really don't need the deli-cious ones, so how about any other variety of your doughnuts? Oh, you're referring to your entire menu as delicious doughnuts? So that means the entire doughnut idea is shot.* This sent me to the grocery store, whose doughnuts pale in comparison. And believe me, I heard complaints about this two-bit second choice from the boys. Never mind that their mother went to two places to find chocolate glazed and maple-cream sticks. Can't we all just get along for the sake of the fact that I was seriously uncomfortable a number of years ago on this anniversary? Epidurals for everyone, I say.

In the end Tucker took a lovely collection of well-dressed cupcakes to school the next morning, middle tier notwithstanding. I stepped up and we did it. The only thing clogged the next morning was the bathtub, which I told myself must operate on an entirely different set of pipes. I ignored the pesky detail that the bathtub clog presented another problem, and I moved on in pleasant, hopeful ignorance that it would just take care of itself.

I did the birthday shopping that afternoon at a place that will wrap gifts for me. I used to wrap gifts—quite beautifully, actually. But that has gone by the wayside along with a million other things I used to do well, like grocery shop and plan a menu and cook. Anyway, I chose airplanes, a collection of football figures, Legos, a couple of Wii games, and a couple of small games that, as always, I think I'll play with the boys when I buy them, and a kit to build your own robots. The box promised "easy assembly." You'd think I would have learned by now.

I have to say that following directions and putting things together is a huge trigger for me. I can feel the anxiety building. It's not that it's a man's job; it's just that in the past it wasn't my job. Robb thought like an engineer, and things like this were so fascinating to him. Now I'm having to understand words like "motor space" and "chassis" and "locate a small screwdriver before you begin." Where the stink is the small screwdriver? And on which blessed side does the chassis go? I tried. I read the directions, I studied the pictures, and Tucker, bless his heart, was so patient. I finally set it all down and said, "I'm sorry, buddy. I can't do this. I'm sorry that I can't."

He put his hands on my shoulder and said, "It's okay, Mommy. Really."

It's just not, though, buddy. It's not. It's your big birthday gift and you can't play with it.

Thankfully, he was appropriately pleased with the Wii games, and he didn't even mind that I hadn't wrapped them. Those happy little surprises distracted everyone until I could find that blessing of a little screwdriver.

Sometimes I am overwhelmed by the many things in my life that are not going the way I wanted or the way I had planned. To change anything feels like turning a massive ship with a small rudder. It's as though I've been given a large marble slab and a chisel. It takes a lot of slow, careful chipping away before it's finished, but I'm banking on the hope that there's a masterpiece hidden underneath. And breaking my nails as I chisel my fingers to the bone.

eight

O n one particular morning, in that brief window when the boys have been authorized to get in the car and I have yet to join them, I heard wailing from the garage—the kind that makes me snap to attention. As I quickly gathered by deductive reasoning (since explanations were sparse), the kitchen door closed behind Tyler, nudging him down the two steps more quickly than he'd planned. No injuries, no smashed fingers, no skinned knees, but two very unhappy boys. Unhappy with me. Really, a better word is *angry*.

Tyler cried, so tearfully and passionately, "You closed the door on me!" And Tucker, ever the faithful protector when it is convenient for his cause, accused, "Mommy, you hurt my brother!"

Okay, no, I didn't. And no, I didn't. I was far from the door when it closed, and while that may be in part their point because I didn't stop it from happening, I most certainly did not allow it with intent.

They were angry. Everything stopped while I clarified in no uncertain terms that I will never, ever hurt my children or let anything bad happen to them on purpose. Understand? Everyone? Repeat it back to me. Clarity is of great importance, gentlemen.

We gathered ourselves, finally accomplished the task of the seat belts, and were on our way.

But the scene stayed with me as I realized how very often I

have let that play out with God in very similar terms. Something comes crashing down on me, shatters nearby, or even gently nudges me faster than I want to go. And on whom do I place the blame? *God! Why did you let that happen? Why did you do that to me? Where were you?*

Of course the parallels have limits; God is omnipotent and omnipresent, and I am assuredly not. Even still, there are things that happen, not because he wishes them to and certainly not because he wasn't paying attention, but merely because things happen. Doors slam, knees are skinned, dreams are delayed, hearts ache. But maybe it's not really his fault at all.

Theology. Born of *theos* and *logy*. "God" and "study." The study of God. In my mind I hear a booming voice resounding against the walls of a high-ceilinged cathedral, saying those words: "The study of God." I think of heavy concordances. I think of books, books, books—countless pages of weighty language. I think of words like *Calvinist, Armenian, postmodern, reformed*. A language all its own. The stuff seminary is made of.

But if theology is the study of God, then isn't that all I am doing? As I seek to make sense of this; as I start a new day and seek to find anything in it at all; as I find hope I can't explain; as my bones ache within me; as joy comes in the morning; as I think and learn and feel; as I process who I am, who Robb was, who we were together, who I am without him, who he is now as a new creation; as I think about the questions my children ask; as I think about the ones I may never be able to answer; as Tucker asks me if I can please give him a baby sister; as I tell him, no, we need a daddy for that; as I wonder if his daddy now knows if our other two children are the sisters Tucker wishes for; as I think about grief, healing, and how it's all depicted in an ocean of grace; as I remember; as I look for God in all this—is this theology?

Studying God in today. Asking the questions. Perhaps I am becoming a theologian, one who studies God.

Each time I was pregnant, I took multiple pregnancy tests, peeing on a new stick over and over again just to make sure it was really, really, for really real, true. Each one showed me two pink stripes, and yet an hour later or two weeks later, I insisted on taking another test. Until I could feel a baby kicking inside me, until I started to outgrow even the rubber-band trick on my jeans, I couldn't believe it was true.

I sang these words to my boys when they were growing inside me. "You're just too good to be true. Can't take my eyes off of you," marveling that this everyday miracle could happen to me.

Even as I lean into what I believe is a gift of faith, I seem to be a girl who needs reminding. Is it true? Still true? How about now?

As I prepared to teach a group of women this week, I was looking closely at a few verses in the first chapter of James. The words that say if you lack wisdom, if you need more of it, ask God. He'll give you more, every time, and he'll give it to you generously. And he won't mind that you asked, and he won't criticize you for not knowing on your own.

But there's a catch: you have to believe you will receive it. The verses say believe and don't doubt. Because she who doubts is like a wave of the sea, blown and tossed by the wind. The verse tells me that if I ask but I don't believe, then I am double-minded. Having two hearts or one divided. Reaching in two separate directions. Asking for Plan A but creating Plan B. Double-minded. (A word that James made up, historians say, which gives me hope for the word *tarbled*.)

Oh my great day. It's so much easier to teach a principle than to practice it, and of course God, in his mercy, would call me to claim the very words he gave me to speak. In my asking and asking "Is it true? Still true? How about now?" I've been double-minded. I've asked for one thing, believed for a moment that it is mine, and then asked God to confirm it yet again.

In essence, it's as if I'm saying as I did years ago, "Give me another pregnancy test. The last one has faded in my mind." It's hard to believe in any or all of this.

There are three options. You can live life as if it's all one big accident of happenstance. Maybe you can live your life as though everything is a bad joke. I can't.

Or you can lie on your trampoline at night and look at the stars and decide they were definitely made by a Creator but he must not care about you or us or this day or this life. He doesn't care, or if he cares, he cares only about the ultimate end of his creation, and he is otherwise indifferent. You don't matter to him, and I don't matter to him, except possibly as a means to an end. I can't live that way either.

There's one other way to live: as though you believe that the universe is powered by love, a personal love that is deeper and bigger than anything you can imagine, and that all of us really do matter to the lover. He loves us so much that our lives matter and our decisions are important; he really does know about the fall of every sparrow, and the hairs of our head are really numbered. Given my choices—and surely we all have them—that's the only way I can live.

I think I'm supposed to put all my eggs in one basket: his. That's what it is to believe and not doubt. I think that's what it is to trust him, no matter what, and to move forward in a promise without asking him to repeat it again and again.

And so it seems I have three baskets.

1. Please, God. I put my faith in you. Here is my every hope and dream.
2. I think you're legit, but just in case you don't come through, I'm keeping my options open.
3. In case you need help fulfilling your promise in my life, I'm happy to step in at any time and make things happen on my own.

Noah built an ark when there was no rain. Mary grew a baby when she had never been with a man (and that was before the days of pink stripes on sticks).

Abraham packed up his wife and started traveling without a map or clear destination. He just knew to go. Faith isn't the absence of doubt, just as courage isn't the absence of fear. Doubt and fear like to climb into the backseat, pretending, assuming, and encouraging each other that they are accepted as passengers for the journey.

God, please help me believe. Give me an undivided heart so that I may know you better. And please forgive me when I think I need to buy another proverbial pregnancy test.

Your stripes are enough. You're always enough.

Part Three

people need spoons

I think one of the most important gifts I can give my children is the truth that they are never alone. I am on their side and in their corner because in this family we choose each other. I don't want them to live in fear of a friend saying, "I'm going to tell your mom," or of a teacher saying, "We will need to call a parent." I mean, I get it. I was a teacher, and I know that parent contact is definitely part of the consequence process. But I'm interested in tilting that axis a bit, to move it from punishment to discipline. Maybe I can help my boys not to view their lives as quite so compartmentalized, with school in one place and home in another, and never the two shall meet. No, I'd like them to know that their teachers and I all stand together on the bandwagon called authority and that if their teachers call me, it isn't to make things worse. It is to make sure we all have the same information since we all have the same goal of helping them grow up to be smart, confident, and helpful.

Sure, there's a healthy fear in the consequence of calling mom. But I hope it's an extension of the healthy fear they have of me anyway, the gut instinct that reminds them I am in charge and we are not peers quite yet. I want them to know "I'm in your corner, on your side, and if there's a consequence at hand, it's because I want what is best for you. I'm on your team. Team you."

This doesn't mean I'll rescue them. It doesn't mean no consequences. But as much as it depends on me, I want my children to never stand alone. As long as they know that, then they can feel free to hate me when I disagree with them. I'm not afraid of an angry kid.

I keep an ear to the ground when they are playing, and I pray for their wisdom and their safety. I know that one day "across the street" may be "across the world," and the life lessons of today will matter then. So I let them play, and I let life and relationships unfold, and then I'm here just in case they need some extra wisdom in their pockets. Or, in some cases, fierce protection.

The boys were playing with a handful of children from our new neighborhood, jumping on the trampoline, shooting hoops, doing the neighborhood do. They tumbled in the door, dripping over each other in a race to be the first to get to me, since the winner of that race would invariably be the first to tell his side of the story. They had gotten in a fight—with each other. Throws and blows.

"He beat me up, Mommy."

"Well, he punched me in the eye."

"That's only because I was afraid."

Yes, lovey. That's called protecting yourself.

But then another detail emerged: the little girls had dared Tuck to beat up his brother. *Stop right there. This is not going down this way.* I had several issues before me: brother violence, family loyalty, bullying, peer pressure, and setting boundaries with kids who follow different rules. I hardly knew where to begin.

I set them on the couch in front of me. They were sweaty in that sticky way boys get. Tuck wore a baseball cap, a football jersey, and cut-off jeans that showed the grass stains on his knees. Tyler wore a stretched-out basketball shirt that hung on his pencil-like frame and matching shorts that came far below his knees.

I explained that "in our family" we do not ever punch or fight. That's not how we solve anything. My heart broke in front of them over the very idea of one brother turning against the other. "Guys, don't you know that you're each other's best friend?"

"What? He's my BFF? I didn't even know that."

Well, I'm glad I brought that to your attention. I'll continue to remind you when you're in doubt. We talked about choosing a brother, always.

"Yeah, even if I do mean things to him, he should still be on my side."

"Well, you shouldn't do mean things to him. That's the nature of being on his side."

And then I knew—I knew that I knew—I needed to wade the raging waters of crossing the street, ringing the doorbell, and having a conversation on my own. I do not love conflict. I do not love confrontation. But I do love my boys. And the ferocity of a mother's courage is unmatched. I confess that I wished for the privilege of sending Robb into the scene. Or the solidarity of saying, "His dad and I have decided . . ." But those were not my options. I needed to step up. These little girls threw my boys into a dogfight just to see what would happen. I thought, *We may be new to the neighborhood, but let me tell you: this is not how it's going to happen around here.*

Tuck rang the doorbell. We waited. We heard scrambling inside. "Dad! It's the neighbors! It's Tucker and Tyler's mom!" *Yeah, it is.* I squared my shoulders and looked at my reflection in the window, trying to strike the balance of intimidating and approachable. Dad came to the door, and I forged into new territory.

"Hi, my name is Tricia, and it's so good to meet you. Can you help me with your name? Oh yes. I remember. Thank you. I just wanted to check in with you tonight. See, my boys were fighting with each other in your yard. I'm dealing with that issue inside our home, since punching and fighting are not allowed. But they both tell me your girls dared them to do it, encouraged them to punch each other. So I just wanted to talk with you to see if that's the story you've heard as well."

He called both girls to the front door. They both confessed. *Yes, we did that. We don't know why. We know it's wrong. We won't anymore.* He sent them to their rooms, grounding them for a day. But as they walked up the stairs, I called to them, "Girls, we love you both, and we love having you over to play. But I need you to know, in our family no punching is allowed. In fact, if you ever see my children hitting or fighting each other, you have my permission to come straight to me. Tell me right away because they are breaking the rules. So please do not ever, ever encourage or dare them to fight with each other or anyone else. I would love to have you over again soon."

And I meant it. In fact, those were two of the neighborhood crew I later recruited to carry my shabby chic, antique, and enormous desk upstairs to my writing studio. I paid them with chocolate. (Yep. Not above it.)

As we stood on their front porch that evening, the girls went to their rooms, and the dad apologized sincerely. He explained that he had worked all day, his wife was traveling, and sometimes he felt like a single parent. And at the end of the day, sometimes he was just too tired to keep track. Yes, I understand how that feels. We shook hands, made eye contact, and I left every ounce of grace behind as we left for our home.

I showed the neighborhood bullies that there's a new sheriff in town. She has snacks in her pantry, chocolate in her purse, and fun in her home. But she has boundaries and rules and a firm voice.

We love you, and you're welcome here, provided you follow the rules.

It was an epic night. Tuck learned the mighty force of peer pressure and how it works. Both boys learned about family loyalty. Tyler learned that he is not alone, that although he is the youngest in the neighborhood and while he is not "a mama's boy," he is not alone.

Later that night as he was brushing his teeth in his fleece jammies, I asked him, "Tyler, what'd you learn about us today?"

He spit a mouthful of toothpaste into the sink and wiped some from his chin. "That you're always in my corner."

"I am, buddy. Always. Who has a fierce mom?"

"I do."

"You sure do."

"And, Mommy? You do too." He's right. I do too. I learned from the best.

I put the boys to bed and fell into my own, too tired to put on my jammies.

My husband and my brother have the same name, spelled differently. My brother is Rob; I married Robb. One *b*, two *b*'s. I know it's tricky. Believe me, it led to many years of confused conversations in our family, as we often didn't realize we weren't talking about the same Rob(b). I tell you this because I'm about to talk about my brother, and I don't want you to get confused and think I'm talking about the man I married. Glad we covered that.

My brother Rob and I are almost two years apart. It doesn't matter as much or at all now that we are thirty-three and thirty-five, but for two decades I held confidently to the twenty-two months between us. The gap felt wider while we were in school, since he was the oldest in his class and I was the youngest in mine. It was the difference between toddler and preschooler, middle school and high school, taking the bus to school or driving, freshman and senior. I felt terribly insecure in those six weeks between May and July, after his birthday but before mine, when he was just one year behind me. Most of the time I could say I was two years older, but for that brief window each year, I felt like he was chasing my heels and nipping at my firstborn rights. During the weeks when he had proudly "just turned ten," I was projecting myself into the future by telling others that I was "nearly twelve."

We are each other's biggest fan. I dig him. People often ask us, "How did you two become such good friends?" Our parents hear a variation of the same: "How did you teach them to do that?" Rob and I faithfully say that our friendship is in large part due to

the environment our parents created at home; our parents faithfully say that our friendship had little to do with them and much
to do with our decisions as siblings. I propose it was a recipe of
both.

Mom and Dad laid some foundational groundwork:

1. No name calling. It's okay to be angry, but it's not
   okay to be mean.

2. No physical violence. Say what you need to say, but do
   not hit, scratch, punch, or pull hair. Ever. (There was
   one serious battle over the TV remote control when
   we were eleven and nine, and our parents followed
   through. No dice. Don't try that again.)

3. Our home was a fun place to be. Our family had fun
   together, we laughed a lot, and these truths caused
   Rob and me to want to come home—and bring our
   friends.

4. While friends were always welcome, there was one
   exception: our family vacations were exclusive to
   our family. We had a getaway once a year, and the
   destination and duration varied based on the state of
   family finances. But there was always a vacation, and
   it belonged only to us. My brother and I were never
   invited to bring a friend along; we were encouraged
   to find friendship in each other. As a result, all our
   favorite memories are mutual—we share them with
   each other, not with a friend or neighbor passing
   through a particular life stage.

Those were the foundational pieces, but please don't be deceived. There were a good many years when we did not enjoy each other at all, and if our only choice was each other, then we chose to play alone and apart. Our affinity didn't come as a birthright; we chose it later on.

When we were fourteen and twelve, we watched our uncle, who was just thirty-three, die a long and slow death. Watching Dad lose his younger brother, Rob and I caught our first glimpse of the fragility of life and the gift of a sibling. We both remember the day we said to each other, "So, hey, how about this: what if we decide to like each other?" We didn't know any other siblings who got along, who truly preferred each other, and we wondered what it might be like to give it a go.

"Friends?"

"Best friends. It starts today."

And we never looked back.

There's no way to get around this, so let me say this first: In the following story I look like the hero. And that's not how I meant for it to go, and that's not why I tell the story right now. But I'm just telling you, that's how it goes. Sorry about that.

My brother and I spent one year in high school together. He was entering the scene as a freshman, and I was wrapping things up as a senior. Rob and I were close, so having a senior in his corner made him a big fish in a little pond. We lived life together that year, and he lived the life of a near-graduate.

Our cafeteria was set up with round tables, so it felt at least in part as if we were eating with some dignity rather than sitting at the troughlike tables with attached benches. The only rule for the round tables: no more than eight chairs. No more. Ever. More than eight chairs was the equivalent of pulling the fire alarm without a real emergency. I mean, there were rumors of isolation and dungeons for the brave fool who added the ninth chair. Rob and I didn't usually get to have lunch together at the same period, so I don't know why this lunch period was the exception. But for some reason, on this day in my memory, he was there, and he was naturally welcome to sit at my table. Except . . . we had nine people at the table. (Shudder. I know.)

The principal patrolled past our table, and with a quick head count, we were busted.

"Ladies and gentlemen, there are too many chairs at this table. Unacceptable. One of you needs to move to a different table immediately."

In classic insubordination we didn't acknowledge his words. We just looked at one another, ate our lunch, and acted as if he might disappear if we pretended to be invisible. No dice. He targeted my brother, the lone freshman at a table of seniors. "Son, you need to move to a different table. Pick another place to sit."

"I was invited to sit here." Rob was respectful and his tone was even.

"Kid, you're a freshman. They are seniors. They can't want you here. Move to a different table."

Still, so respectful, he said, "She's my sister." It's the only explanation he or I needed for most of the questions in our lives. *He's my brother. She's my sister.* That's all there was to it.

In retrospect I think the principal was aiming to earn a few points with the seniors, clearing out the riffraff among our elite lunch table. He pointed to my brother and gestured to the table behind us. A long rectangular table. Empty and troughlike. He was sentencing my brother to the ultimate indignity in a high school cafeteria: to eat alone. Rob picked up his lunch tray and gave one more plea. "She's my sister." The principal repeated the gesture, and my brother had been dismissed from my circle of friends.

Before Rob took one step away from the table, I picked up my lunch tray. "I'll join you, Rob," I said. And as I stepped around the principal, I said, "Please excuse me. I'd like to have lunch with my brother." We took seats on either side of the table, across from each other, and we continued our lunch and our conversation.

What was the alternative? To stay with my friends? To watch my brother—or ignore my brother—as he sat by himself a few feet from me but miles away in his heart? Even now the mental image of my brother sitting alone in that cafeteria can bring me to tears. I just couldn't let that happen. There was no other option.

That story has become famous in our family history, and it's an example of our family values: in our family we choose one another. As long as you're in this family, you'll never be alone.

I received my fair share of warnings when it became clear to me and everyone else that I would be raising two boys. "You know, Tricia, you and your brother are an anomaly. Siblings aren't really like that in real life. We don't understand how you two found such chemistry, but it was a lucky strike. So don't plan on duplicating it—especially not with two boys. The odds were in your favor with opposite genders, but when the siblings are both boys? Well, good luck striking a chord of friendship between the two of them. I'm not saying it's impossible. I'm just saying don't get your hopes up."

First of all, those are miserable things to tell someone. Those sentiments are almost as miserable as the one expressed by the woman who met me in an elevator when Tucker was six weeks old. She leaned in and said to me, "Always take pictures of his accidents and injuries before you take him to the ER. He will love you for it." Let me tell you, I had no intention of allowing any accidents or injuries to happen to the swaddled baby in my arms, he who still had that newborn scent and a scab from his umbilical cord. My postpartum hormones were thrown into orbit by this woman who suggested that something could happen to my son that could cause him pain.

On a side note, I took pictures the first time he broke his arm (before he turned two), and I've established quite a record of photos of the atrocities against his body—and he's only nine. Yes, it turns out she was right; these are his favorite pictures to study and revisit. Still, there are some likelihoods one mom doesn't need to share with another. It's possible that my children will not have a friendship that stands the test of time. I know many siblings who don't enjoy each other, who can finish an entire Thanksgiving dinner without a word to each other. But as much as it depends on me, I will do my best to instill friendship between these two brothers. At least I'll give it a try.

There is the same difference in Tucker's and Tyler's ages as there is in Rob's and my age, but my sons have been made twins by tragedy. They were not born together, but they are being re-birthed together into what is new for all of us. They are learning to complement each other's strengths and weaknesses. Tucker leans on Tyler's verbal skills, and Tyler leans on Tucker's physical strength. They take care of each other, watch out for each other, speak for each other, and live in each other's world. Each one shows his greatest confidence when his brother is on the scene. Many children use their names as a compound word: Tuckertyler. Just yesterday when they woke up, Tyler's first words were "Hey, Tuck, remember that dream we just had?" And they launched into a dialogue of all that had happened while they were sleeping. They belong to each other.

Twenty years have passed since that scene with my brother in the high school cafeteria, and I watched a similar story unfold with my boys. They have a school playmate whom they both enjoy, and the three of them play together on the playground during their shared recess. Odd numbers are usually a challenge in children's circles of play, and this was no exception. On one grouchy day the little boy announced that only Tyler would be his friend. Tuck had come home crying, feeling unwelcome and unwanted. I helped him with those emotions and reminded him that he doesn't have to be with anyone who doesn't want him and that he's way more valuable than that. I let him be angry, and I let him decide that he would never play with this boy again.

I suspected Tucker might change his mind eventually, but I want to give my children a voice. He was angry and hurt, and he was drawing conclusions that weren't hurting anyone, so I didn't need to disagree with him. He didn't need an argument. He needed unconditional agreement: I agree with you, buddy. That wasn't kind.

Tyler was invited to a play date at the little boy's house, and he quietly decided he would rather stay home. "No, thank you. Maybe another time." These were his answers.

But then an invitation came for both of them.

Tucker stood by his hurt feelings and his firm convictions, adding some dramatic flair to his insistence that he would never play with that boy on the playground, at the park, on a train, or on a plane. No way. "Then I'm not going either," Tyler said. "I don't want to hurt Ben's feelings, but I'm not going if Tucker isn't."

It was an interesting position for Tyler, a position of power that a younger sibling rarely gets. He could go and let his brother feel excluded. He could carry the coveted title of wanted friend. But it didn't occur to him. Apparently this wasn't even an option on his radar.

Weeks passed, and my children came home from school with tales of playing together or alone on the playground but never with Ben. Tyler's strong will worked in his favor, and he would not give an inch—until one morning on the way to school when Tucker suggested they give Ben another chance.

"Are you sure?" Tyler asked. "Because I only want to if you want to."

"I'm sure. Let's forgive him."

There are some things I don't know how to teach them, and there's a good bit in this story that has nothing to do with anything I've taught them. But there's one thing I learned long before they were born: in our family we choose one another.

ten

Hospitality was always a bone of contention for Robb and me. When it came to opening our doors to the world, we were yin and yang. I was ever the party girl, always willing and ready to fill our every weekend—and some weeknights— with dinners, game nights, time slots and obligations, appetizers and desserts. He craved the privacy of our home, the sprawling possibilities of an open weekend, and a comfy evening to settle in front of the TV and watch football or baseball or poker. We learned from each other; I taught him how to have fun, and he showed me how to mellow. I brought sunshine to his calendar while he brought the gravity that kept me from spinning into space.

He was a minimalist while I found love in the abundance of details, so we didn't naturally plan a party the same way. But in order to throw the parties I loved, I learned to curb my tendencies so they would fit within his comfort zone. I planned within a budget, put things on the calendar well in advance, and had a clearly defined guest list. And if I could manage to be ready before the first guests rang the doorbell, then I could assuage his anxiety, and he could settle down to enjoy himself. Unfortunately, I never mastered that last part; it seems I was always putting away the vacuum cleaner or setting the table or just not behaving with a sense of urgency. So hospitality was always something of a bone to pick between the two of us. But that's what marriages are made of:

the habits you wish to change and the quirks you learn to live with. Or without.

See, the thing is, I grew up in a home with an open door. My brother and I were always, always encouraged to bring home our friends—any number of them—at any hour of the day or night. As a teenager, I loved this social perk, and as a mom, I recognize the added benefits: our parents always knew where we were and the people we were with. Some of my girlfriends from high school recall a time when they serenaded me outside my window in the wee small hours of the morning of my birthday. And though the crowd was unexpected and the sun wouldn't come up for hours, my parents invited them all inside and whipped together a snack buffet of Popsicles and cheese puffs. This is the home I grew up in: there's always room for more, and the people you love are welcome here.

I used to worry about how I would instill in my boys a love for hospitality if my husband and I weren't on the same page. I imagined our boys as teenagers, their friends surprising us in the middle of the night just as my friends had surprised my parents. While I knew I would want to throw open the doors and pour all the snacks onto the coffee table, I could envision Robb wanting to call the police in a fury over being awakened by trespassers. How could I love as my parents had loved? How could I teach my children such openness and spontaneity while also respecting their dad's need for structure and privacy—and sleep?

But then life took a turn that none of us saw coming, and with the trauma of Robb's death, the flame of my spontaneity blew out like a birthday candle. I developed chronic anxiety; I became an agoraphobic introvert. Suddenly Robb's preferences made more sense to me. I became the one who needed structure, privacy, and sleep. Still, I love the model and the message of hospitality, so I push myself in the ways I once pushed Robb. I put dates on the calendar, and we plan and prepare. The tables have turned; now my boys bring the sunshine, and I bring the gravity. I had spent all those early years worrying how I would ever work around Robb's social stuffiness, but in the end my own social apprehension became the greatest hindrance of all.

I did not see that coming.

When someone has dinner at our home for the first time, we serve this guest on our red plate. It truly doesn't matter people's age or whose guest they are, which means that my friends get the royal treatment too. In our family we are equal-opportunity "celebrationists." If you're joining us for the first time, the red plate is yours. And at your red-plate dinner, the rest of us get to ask you questions of our choice. Don't think firing squad; think opportunity to shine, for you to talk all about yourself without apology, for my children to learn how to be good conversationalists, and for all of us to learn about someone new.

I grew up with this tradition and happen to know from longitudinal studies that it lends itself well to dating relationships also. Our family's culture is growing accustomed to honoring someone new with engaging conversation, so when my boys are teenagers, the idea of introducing new people to our family won't be a jarring culture shift. In that life stage, if my boys prefer, we can stop using the actual red plate, since it's really only a prop for the actual tradition. It's never too early to start thinking about such transitions, so I am told.

When the boys hosted their first red-plate dinner, they each brought a friend home from school: a precocious little boy and a lovely "friend who is a girl." I served pizza and grapes and Kool-Aid. (Tucker's little buddy guest asked me if it was alcohol.) We shared our questions around the table. These included "What is your favorite color? What is your favorite dessert? What is your favorite weapon?" But Tyler nixed that one, since it isn't appropriate to talk about violence and weapons unless a girl wants to. He carried her plate for her and refilled her drink, and he ordered the other boys to stop making up stories about their imaginary friend, Mr. Poopy Farty Diaper Head.

"Hey. There's a lady here, you guys."

And thus began the passing of the hospitality baton. *Well done, little mosquitoes.*

My cupboards are open for the boys to share with their friends, and there's nothing we have that we love too much to give away. There is always more where this came from, and when we're not sure, we give it away . . . anyway. I want the boys to know that everything we have is for sharing.

It was springtime, with the lengthening of days and the end of the school year quickly approaching. I was sitting at the top of our stairwell in my jammies, talking on the phone to my long-distance and lifelong friend Laurelyn. As I chatted, the boys came in and out, in and out, in and out. They were perpetually annoyed that I was still on the phone instead of serving dessert. Finally Tucker brought me a half gallon of ice cream and asked me to take off the lid. He had resolved to solve this problem on his own. I applauded this mentality because I love strides of independence, and I continued my phone conversation with Laurelyn.

Then came a few more trips in and out, now with a grocery bag. And then he passed by with my silverware drawer in his hands. The whole drawer.

"Hold on one second, Laur." I put my hand over the receiver and called to my son, "Tuck? What are you doing with the silverware?"

He looked up the stairs and said as a matter of fact, "Mommy, people need spoons."

And he strode out the door, drawer in hand.

"Laur, I'll call you right back. I've got some kind of a . . . spoon situation here." Oh, the random and questionable happenings to a mom of boys while she talks on the phone.

I followed my son outside and found a dozen children in my front yard, ranging from first grade to eleventh, and ice-cream shrapnel scattered all around. Three tubs of ice cream—one vanilla and two mint chocolate chip—all the sprinkles from the baking cupboard, an array of plastic plates and cups, and my silverware drawer. Five teenagers sat on the front porch, in rocking chairs and on the ground, texting and laughing and telling their summertime sagas. Girls were braiding hair. Boys were shooting hoops.

There was laughter. There was community. And my sons were covered in ice cream up to their elbows as they scooped one bowl after another.

"Hey, everybody, looks like quite a party out here!"

"Hi, Tucker and Tyler's mom! Thanks for the ice cream!"

"You bet, guys. I'll stay stocked all summer. You're welcome here anytime."

At 9:47 I called my two children inside. And I'd like to say that I think 9:47 is entirely generous for a six- and a seven-year-old. The party continued in the front yard long after I had called the hosts inside. I told the neighborhood crowd that they could stay as late as they wanted, anytime. "I'll leave the porch light on. Good night, everybody. You're my favorite."

One of the girls said, "I'm writing that in my journal tonight."

"It's going on my Facebook wall," said another.

A Costco membership is a small price to pay for my children's favor among their friends. As a bonus, there is community, friendship, love, and sprinkles.

All on my front porch.

"Tonight's dinner question is, what's the hardest thing you've ever done?" We are fans of TableTopics, the family edition. Their clever questions relieve the great burden I feel for teaching my children to make dinner conversation when it's the end of the day and my own words are few. TableTopics keeps us from resorting to TV trays and SpongeBob.

Tucker said, "Painting a thousand houses." We clarified that this is the hardest thing he can think of doing since he hasn't actually done it. That's fair.

My dad said, "Studying and taking the exam to become a licensed clinical social worker."

My mom said, "When I went to visit Uncle Rob when he lived in Japan. We needed to get off the plane in a country where we couldn't speak the language, then take three subways and two buses on which we couldn't read the signs, and then we needed to navigate walking directions to the hotel Rob had sent us to. If we got it right, he would be there an hour later. But if we got it wrong, there was no way to find him."

"Did you find him, Grandma?" Their eyes were wide with anticipation.

"We did." She smiled. "But it was a scary day."

It was my turn. I wanted to think of something clever, but I couldn't.

I said, "The hardest thing I've ever done is learning to live and be happy again after Daddy died."

And Tyler finished our circle. "My hardest thing is trying to make Mommy happy when she's sad from missing Daddy."

Thank you, sweet boy. May you someday understand that if you've helped to mend a broken heart, you have had expert training for many of the hard things that will come your way as a man.

eleven

If you think your kids eat a lot of McDonald's food, I'm pretty sure I can put your mind at ease when I tell you I think mine eat more. I'm not going to tell you how often we eat there each week because I can't bring myself to say it out loud. But let's just say we're on a first-name basis with many of the employees, my children have played many times with the little boy who hangs out at the corner booth while his mom is working, and I know the exact change required for two Happy Meals with chocolate milk and a number-two value meal, hold the cheese.

Plus, there's Wi-Fi, outlets for my computer, and bottomless refills of the very best Diet Coke in all the land. I'm telling you, that's pretty much all I need for days on end.

"Looks like it's a Happy Meal day, and everybody knows a Happy Meal day is a great day!" the old man said as we sat in a booth near him. His face looked like leather and his cheeks were sunken, but his voice was jovial and his eyes sparkled. He counted out quarters and dimes he had spilled onto the tabletop. When I saw the blankets and coats piled next to him in his booth, I realized I'd seen him before: on the corner of the exit from the highway. He stood his post day after day, but I stopped only if I knew the light was about to turn green (briefly, in other words) and I had a granola bar to share from inside my purse.

Tyler had often asked me, "Mommy, why didn't you give that

man all the money you have? You have money in your purse. Why didn't you give it to him if he's hungry?" The truth of helping people seems so clear, but the answers of discernment often seem so complicated. Robb hated, hated, hated when I approached people who live on the streets. He reminded me often that the world is no longer the safe cul-de-sac of suburbia that I had grown up in, and he had always pleaded with me not to take such risks. I conceded by not giving away money, only food, and by keeping my foot above the gas pedal to make a quick getaway if I needed to.

But here we were, at McDonald's, and in the next booth was the man I had seen so many times. I really cannot convey this enough: He wasn't strange or scary. He was just hungry. When he gathered his change and started toward the counter, I followed him. I put my hand on his shoulder and slipped two fives into his hand. "Here you go, sir."

He looked at me with light in his eyes. "Thank you, ma'am. Thank you very much."

Honestly, in every sense of the cliché, it was the least I could do. I couldn't just sit there with my well-dressed kids in their brand-new back-to-school shoes while they let food go to waste because they were more interested in playing on expensive and unnecessary technology that I take with me everywhere. Embarrassed by my own excess, I could at least buy his lunch.

While he waited for his food, I leaned in close to the boys and whispered to them. "Guys, the man who was sitting next to us doesn't have a home or any money, so I shared some of our money with him to buy his lunch today."

They looked over at his booth, noticing this time the load the man carried, including his cardboard sign asking for handouts. "Are you afraid of him, Mommy?"

"I'm not afraid at all. There's a place in the Bible where Jesus said that if we give a glass of water to someone who is thirsty, it makes Jesus just as happy as if we had given the water directly to Jesus himself. Today I know that this man just needs some lunch, and we can buy that for him."

I prepped them for when he would return to the table; I told them not to stare at him but to treat him with dignity. He's a man who has less than we have, and we can give him our respect. Sure enough, he came back to the table with a soft drink, a hamburger, and an ice-cream cone.

In honor of the beginning of Broncos season, the Happy Meal toys were football figurines in various poses of the game. Naturally, Tyler handed his over to Tucker, demonstrating his total lack of personal interest in the sport. We unfolded the chart that came with the football players, and we checked off the teams he had collected up to this point. I said, "Tuck, wouldn't it be fun if you could memorize each of their poses? Like, look what that one's doing—reaching to catch the ball."

Tucker found inspiration before I even finished my sentence and stood and mimicked the guy in the picture, showing me he could.

The man next to us spoke again, his voice and diction crystal clear. "Well, young man, you look like a Heisman Trophy winner when you do that. Are you a football player?"

Tuck's chin rose with confidence. Clearly, someone had recognized his calling. "Yes sir. I am."

"Well then, young man, can you tell me who won the Heisman this year?"

When Tuck didn't know, the man regaled us with stories of the Heisman winners of the last three years, which teams they had played for, and where each had gone to college. One story led him to another, and he told us one statistic after another as well as tales of football players before they were discovered. He was so excited to engage in conversation, and his mind was sharp even as ice cream dripped down his chin.

I asked him, "You are such an expert! Did you play football?"

"No ma'am, I was always too small. But I was a diver. That was my hobby, my sport. In fact, have you ever been to Casa Bonita?"

Now, let me tell you, this got the boys' attention! Casa Bonita is one of the last great vestiges of Denver's most eccentric restaurants. It's a Mexican restaurant boasting "the greatest show in Denver" and "mouth-watering Mexican food," both statements open to debate. But the restaurant is a hit with kids, and its claim to fame is the indoor thirty-foot waterfall and the cliff divers. And on that afternoon, sitting before us was an honest-to-goodness, real-life Casa Bonita cliff diver. I watched the boys' eyebrows raise as the man's credibility grew several notches in their estimation. He was almost a celebrity as far as they were concerned.

Conversation continued, mostly with football trivia, and it became more and more clear to me that this impromptu lunch date would have no natural ending unless I wrapped things up. I began to gather our trash and pile it on the tray, hoping to somehow make a gracious exit from the only conversation the man would probably have all day.

Before I had finished gathering all our mess, the man was standing next to us, reaching for the tray. "Here. Please let me take care of that for you." He shuffled to the trash can. His T-shirt hung on his small frame, his hiking boots were worn and unlaced, and his jeans were gathered and bunched around his waist with a tattered belt that was too big. And he was serving my family.

I asked the boys to refill my cup before we left, since I am nothing if not a frugal maximizer of Diet Coke. While they were at the soda fountain, I walked to the man's table and extended my hand to shake his.

"My name is Tricia. What is your name?"

"My name is Dave, ma'am." He shook my hand with both of his. "God bless you, Tricia. Those are good boys. You take good care of them."

"Thank you, Dave. I'm doing my very best. It was our pleasure to have lunch with you today."

His grip tightened as he remembered one more thing to tell me before I slipped out of his life, maybe forever. "Tricia? Make sure they know the book of Philippians, okay? The fourth chapter."

I felt the gripping chill of goose bumps down my arms; Robb's favorite Bible passage was from Philippians 4. He had memorized much of it in college, and he had claimed Philippians 4:13 as his life verse: "I can do all things through Christ who strengthens me."

"Dave, I love the book of Philippians."

As my children returned to the table, sneaking forbidden sips from my straw before they gave my cup to me, Dave turned to them and began reciting scripture with the charisma of a practiced storyteller. "Always be glad because of the Lord! I will say it again:

be glad. Always be gentle with others, for the Lord will soon be here. And remember: don't worry about anything, but pray about everything. With thankful hearts, offer your prayers and requests to God. And because you belong to Christ Jesus, God will bless you with peace that no one can completely understand. Boys, always remember that the Lord your God will give you the strength to face anything he asks you to do. God bless you, boys. Take care of your mom."

Two thoughts came to my mind as I staggered under the weight of the moment. I recalled pounding my fists on the floor of my closet after Tyler's Tae Kwon Do incident, begging my God to show me he was near. And I wondered if perhaps I had just had lunch with an angel sent on a mission.

Part Four

just different

twelve

M ommy, I need more blanket."
    I didn't even know that my boy with the marigold
hair was sleeping next to me. Tyler came sometime during the
night. He had completed a row on his sticker chart and earned a
new Captain America toy for five consecutive nights in his own
bed, but he tells me now that what scares him most are the crabs
and spiders that climb out of his dreams. Such is the sleep cycle of
a young artist. Creatures meet him in his sleep.

"Sure, buddy. Mommy's here." *And I don't let spiders into my
bed. You're safe here.*

He fell back to sleep, and I slipped out of bed to start the day
before both of them. When I can swing it, that always feels like a
bonus head start. I stood in the warm shower, enjoying silence and
fixing my thoughts on truth as I pieced together any Scripture
that came to my mind. Sometimes it's refreshing not to try to recall chapters and verses but simply to think about the words.

> *Let the morning bring me word of your unfailing love,*
> *for I have put my trust in you.*
> *Show me the way I should go,*
> *for to you I lift up my soul.*

Establish the work of my hands, O Lord.
Not to us, but to your Name be the glory.

"Stop kicking me!"

Morning has broken . . . is broken?

"I need more blanket!"

"I don't like your breath!"

"My breath isn't anywhere near you!"

"Move over!"

"*You* move over!"

It sounds like they're awake. I call to them, "That blanket was big enough to cover Daddy and me. It's big enough to cover the two of you. Find a way to fit if you're going to lie there."

I am nearly ready before I step into their morning dance. It's hard when they start the day fighting; it's like waking up to a loud, buzzing alarm. It makes me a little grumpy.

"Good morning, guys. Let's get you dressed."

"I don't want to get dressed. Ever. Zero dressed."

"Tyler, you need to. It's what people do. Tucker, it's Silly Day in your class today. Let's pick out some silliness for you to wear." Tucker finds a Hawaiian lei, a Lightning McQueen hat, and fuzzy slipper socks with green and blue stripes. Silly: check.

Tyler has taken a framed picture of Robb from the credenza in my office. It's of a seventeen-year-old Robb, a picture from his senior year in high school. Handsome Robb. Tucker looks so much like him. Tyler is carrying it around, hoarding and teasing. The older brother whines, "But I want to see the picture too!"

The little brother is in the corner of the bedroom, between the bed and the wall, his eyebrows furrowed in knots. "No. I'm holding Daddy." I am torn. Is his heart wrapped around a picture of Robb, or is the greater joy in having something he doesn't want to share?

"Tyler, please share it with Tucker. That's his daddy too."

"I don't want him to touch it."

"He won't touch it. Just show him."

"I'll touch it," Tucker says defiantly.

"Give me the picture, Tyler." I strike a happy medium, holding the picture Tyler doesn't want Tucker to hold and letting Tucker study the red hair and sturdy jaw line of his dad. The room is silent for just a few seconds.

"My daddy," Tuck whispers.

"My picture!" Tyler stomps.

Mommy's picture, really. It's a good thing I like you both.

I divide and conquer, sending them to get dressed at opposite ends of the upstairs. I go downstairs to let out Murphy, the dog, only to find a flood of yellow in the bathroom where he sleeps.

Well, shoot. I didn't make it down fast enough to let him outside before the urge hit. That was one full bladder for such a small dog. Bummer. I gather paper towels, Resolve for pet stains, Lysol, and Clorox wipes, wishing I had remembered to get more Swiffer WetJet solution yesterday at Wal-Mart. *Ah, make do, Tricia. Just clean and sterilize. The boys need breakfast.*

I kneel, a silver sunflower dancing on my beaded pearl necklace, my white sundress brushing against the wood floor. I try not to get it wet in this mess of yuck.

"Mommy, I don't like these."

"You don't like what?"

"These."

"I can't see you. I can't see what you don't like."

"Then come upstairs."

"Tuck, Murph made a big mess on the floor. I'm cleaning it up. Please come here and show me what you're talking about."

He appears behind me. "Hi, buddy. What do you not like?"

"Um, I don't remember."

"It sounded like 'Crocs' or 'socks' or 'rocks in a box.'"

"Oh. These socks. I don't like these. They make me trip."

"Okay. You don't have to wear them."

"I don't want to wear the flowers on my neck either."

"What about the Lightning McQueen hat?"

"No, I don't want to."

"But it's Silly Day."

"But I don't want to."

I understand this dichotomy. I remember it well. I suspect an idea was born in his head, but now he's not sure if his classmates' silly ideas will match his courage. Better to lie low than to stand out when confidence wanes. *I respect that, kiddo.*

"That's up to you, Tuck. You don't have to. Can you help me with breakfast?"

"Yes. Let's do Pop-Tarts." He roots through the pantry while

I throw away the mess of paper towels. He pulls a stool over to the toaster while I wash my hands, again. The toaster is jammed with broken Pop-Tarts gone awry from other mornings. I begin exploratory surgery. I retrieve two of them, but one is smashed into the bottom of the toaster, and pulling out the tray underneath only scatters crumbs everywhere across the counter. No dice on retrieving the Pop-Tart. Unsuccessful surgery.

"Tuck, let's put the Pop-Tarts in the microwave."

"But I need scissors to open them."

"Just give them here. I'll open them." I insist on opening them myself, plating them myself, putting them in the microwave—myself. I am all about empowering, but, honestly, sometimes I just need to get the task done. Independence is a treasured commodity in our house; sometimes it's hard to know who wants it more.

"Tyler, can you come downstairs, please?" No word from Tyler. It crosses my mind that some silent tragedy has perhaps happened upstairs, since that has happened in our home and my mind no longer naturally claims optimism or defaults to truth. I decide to give him one minute to come downstairs before I race upstairs, prepared to call 911. Maternal instincts are not always reasonable, but neither is posttraumatic stress. I hear him coughing as he comes down the stairs. Ah, there we go. Coughing means breathing.

"Ready for breakfast, Tyler?"

"I need markers."

"We're not doing markers. Do you want a Nutri-Grain bar or a Pop-Tart?"

"Can I have gum?"

"No."

"But I found this piece upstairs. I want it." It's Robb's gum. One piece left in my office drawer.

"We're having breakfast, Tyler. It's not time for gum." I choose not to be sentimental about the Spearmint Extra. I simply choose to tell Tyler no, not now. He is angry that he cannot have gum, then angry that I offered cherry Nutri-Grain instead of raspberry, when he knows he chose raspberry at Wal-Mart yesterday, and I realize I said the wrong thing. I meant raspberry. He chooses a Pop-Tart.

"Mommy," Tucker calls, "my foot is bleeding." He holds his foot in his hand, twisting his ankle sideways so I can see between his toes on the underside of his foot. A blister is healing after he hiked in flip-flops because I forgot to pack tennis shoes.

"It looks like it's getting better, Tuck."

"But it's bleeding. Why would God send blood? Why would God do that to me?"

We are dangerously close to a dialogue about the sovereignty of God in relation to a blister between his toes, and this is a topic I feel particularly uneasy about these days. "Tuck, God doesn't do things to hurt us. If it's bleeding, it might be just because it's bleeding."

"Or it could be because I picked at it."

"Yes. Yes, it could be because you picked at it. Does anyone want blueberries?" The boys are now perched on their tall chairs at the table. They cheer for blueberries.

I carry the Tupperware bowl to the table, open the cover, and offer them each a handful of blue to set alongside their brown sugar–cinnamon, no longer fresh from the microwave.

Tyler takes the Tupperware lid for his plate. "Tyler, I need that to keep the blueberries fresh."

"Well, I need it to keep my blueberries off the table."

"That's what your plate is for."

I tilt the seal and let the blueberries spill onto his plate, rolling around the perimeter of the Pop-Tart. I close up the Tupperware bowl, pressing firmly in the center of the seal, just like my Tupperware mom taught me when I was Tucker's age. It cracks and breaks in my hand. *Seriously?* My mind races through the knowledge I have about Tupperware replacements, the pieces Robb had set aside to be replaced—where did he put them, who was the sales consultant he had talked to . . . *Oh, for crying out loud!* I get another seal from the cupboard.

"Mommy, I sat on a blueberry."

"Clean it up, please."

"You clean it up."

"I will not. The napkins are over there. Please clean it up."

"It's okay. I'm full anyway," he says, pointing to the two missing bites. "My teacher says I only have to eat a little."

"True. But I think your tummy is probably still hungry. Plus, you asked for blueberries. I need you to eat them if you ask for them."

I join the boys at the table with my bowl of Raisin Bran Crunch, just in time to see Tyler toss a blueberry squarely into Tucker's glass of milk. Two points.

"Tyler, go sit on the rug by the door. We don't throw food."

As he's sitting on the rug by the door, he peruses his backpack and packed lunch that are sitting by the door. "Mom, I don't want a banana. And I like Captain America fruit snacks better than Alvin and the Chipmunks. Mommy, there's a folder in my backpack for you."

"I know, buddy. I looked at it last night."

"But it's in my backpack again."

"That's because your teachers asked us to send it back on Friday."

"But there's a note in it."

"Right. It's for your teacher."

He left the folder on the floor. He left the banana on the table. He exchanged his fruit snacks for the preferred. And he left remnants of all his undoings. Three minutes before we were to leave the house!

I packed that lunch for him, for heaven's sake. And I sorted through the folder and the notes and papers therein. And he undid it all. New rule: Once your backpack is zipped, no unzipping until you get to school. Unless you are prepared to take responsibility for all that is within and without. And I don't think you are.

Back in the trenches of babies and toddlers, I used to study the moms of older children with such adoration. They seemed to travel so light with their independent children and their hands free of diaper bags and strollers. I wanted it to get easier, and I wanted them to promise me it would. They often told me it doesn't get easier; it just gets different. On the upside I didn't change any diapers this morning, and I didn't have a child climbing in and out of the dishwasher as I filled it after breakfast. I understand what the parents of school-age children have meant all this time: it doesn't get easier; it's just different.

It's Saint Patrick's Day, so I decide to change the subject and embrace the teachable moment. "So when someone asks you today if you are Irish, what will you say?"

"I will say yes, and my great-great-great-great-grandparents died there."

"Well, they lived there. That's what we're focusing on."

"And I have Irish blood. Even though that's gross."

"Do you know what it means to have Irish blood?"

"No. It's gross."

"Well, there's some blood inside you that God used to make you. It's my blood, and I have Irish relatives, and so you have some of that Irish blood in you."

"Your blood. Is . . . is in me?" He shuddered.

"It's only a little."

He shuddered again.

"Anyway, I don't think you're right, Mommy. God makes people from dirt."

"Well, yes, he made the first person from dirt. But after the first person, then he . . . had a few more options. Let's see. What would the Irish say right now? They were big on blessings."

I try to think of one on the fly, right here at the kitchen table.

"Let the wind be at your back, and the sky over your head. And may good things be under your feet. And may shamrocks and leprechauns follow you all the days of your life."

He glances at me. The same look I gave my mom thirty years ago when we were having these conversations. And still I persist, just as my mom persisted.

"Do you want me to sing some Irish songs for you this morning?"

"No. No *thanks,* I mean."

That's actually a good thing because the only ones I know were on my grandma's jukebox in her home. And it's possible that I've woven some non-Irish ditties from that same jukebox into my mental collection. So I may not be entirely reliable on Irish music history.

Another boy is putting on his shoes, and he finds a wayward wasp flying in the room, even though it's barely warm enough for them to want to come out, and I think they've been tricked as we all are by the charms of early spring.

"Wasp! Wasp!" he yells.

"Wasp? A White Anglo-Saxon Protestant? Well, how appropriate on this day—and I hope he's wearing orange!" I crack myself up. All by myself. Moving on . . . "So today when people talk about being Irish . . ."

"I'll tell them your gross blood is in me."

I'm wishing I had finished my makeup and hair before I stepped onto this mommy dance floor this morning. Time is running out. Tucker cleans up the splashes of milk from the blueberry score, Tyler whines on the rug, and I eat a few bites of fiber with raisins.

It's after eight. I'm running late. I dismiss Tyler from the rug.

I dismiss Tucker from the table. I turn on Nick Jr., my fellow parent for the next ten minutes.

I rush upstairs, diffuse the curly mop, brush on some mascara and eyeliner, and slide my feet into flip-flops. I grab the gray "classic piece" cardigan since Starbucks is cold. So is iced soy chai. I come down the stairs to find Tyler spraying Lysol across the wood floor.

"I'm spraying for ants," he tells me. Way to go, super mom. Leave the toxic stuff on the floor. Let him go crazy with it.

"Tyler, stop. Go wash your hands. Tucker, shoes."

Tucker is standing on his tiptoes on top of a stool, reaching above the refrigerator to retrieve Spider-Man from the basket that is called toy jail. I'm about finished with this morning. I really, really am.

"Tucker, get down. Put on shoes. And put the stool away."

"But I—"

"Please, just do it."

Tyler says, "I think we should call it a stool-aid. That rhymes with Kool-Aid."

"I think you should put on your shoes, Tyler. Tuck, shoes and stool."

"She meant shoes and stool-aid, Tuck. That's what we're calling it now."

Oh, my word. I'm living this.

Somehow we make it into the car. I'm not really sure how that happened; the details are a blur. The boys argue over who gets first music choice. Then they argue if VeggieTales are real since pandas are. Then Tucker realizes we are on our way to school and he isn't wearing a single silly thing for silly day.

And at some point I realize that I have kept up with them this morning. And that's a really, really big deal.

It's not easier; it's just different.

thirteen

T hat's-a-snake-that's-a-snake-that's-a-snake." Tucker said it three times, smashing all the words together. I had driven them home from school, and we were pulling into the driveway, and just on the edge of the sidewalk, between the basketball hoop and the driveway, was the biggest snake I've ever seen outside the zoo. A neighbor told me later, "It's just a bull snake. They don't even have teeth." Which, by the way, yes, they do—four rows of them, no less. And anyway, I don't care if it's called Fluffy and blows kisses. It's a snake, and that means I can't handle it.

I pivoted the car in half circles, in and out of the driveway, circling the snake and watching for any movement at all. We must have looked ridiculous, but I had to know if it was alive, and I sure wasn't getting any closer for investigation. I wanted an accelerator firmly under my foot, ready for me to flee the situation.

The snake never moved. Still, I didn't trust him one bit. I parked the car in the garage, we slowly got out with the innate awareness that snakes feel vibrations in the ground, and the three of us kept a safe distance and compared solutions to the problem at hand. I really just wanted to get back in the car for the rest of my life. Tyler felt like we should throw rocks at the snake to make it wake up and go away, but Tucker envisioned it heading straight for us. Perhaps we overestimated the motor skills and agility of the snake, but I was taking no risks. Tyler suggested we make a mad rush at the snake, believing in strength in numbers; I was pretty much willing to stay in the car until the apocalypse.

Tuck called us to attention. "Listen to me. We are going to get in the car, and we are going to go somewhere else. We are not going near the snake, and we will not throw rocks at it. We will leave it alone. We will get in the car, and we will leave." He pointed to the car and raised his eyebrows with an expression that dared us to question him. His voice wavered and his face was pale; he was terrified, but he was determined to take care of his family.

Tuck spoke with such authority that Tyler and I felt compelled to obey. Plus, his plan was infinitely better than ours. We got back in the car, and I did a few more pivots at the end of the driveway to somehow get a closer look at the snake without really touching him or risking my life. Still, the snake never moved.

I drove to McDonald's. I only knew that we needed ice cream, and I would figure the rest out later.

In the rearview mirror I looked at my brave sons, and I found myself talking to Robb in my mind. *Oh, Robb, he's you. Tucker is you! That is your face, your tone. This is how you would tackle the situation and take everyone in hand. How did Tucker learn this from you? How does he know what you would do when he never watched you do this? Wait . . . Tucker didn't learn this. It's his implicit nature. It's who he is. He's operating out of instinct right now—the instinct he shared with you, his dad.*

I recalled so many times when Robb took a matter in hand, when he took the lead, when he rallied a group that needed a leader. So many of those times I had found him overbearing and a little too controlling. I like to think on my own, and I bristle when I feel as if someone—anyone—is getting too close to what I believe is my right to make decisions. I was pretty sure he was trying to make me fall in line with his way of thinking, to make me a girl of caution and details, order and routines.

But no, I realized as I waited at a stoplight and looked at Tuck's profile in the mirror. Robb wasn't trying to control me. He wasn't aiming to restrict or offend me; it's just that he was married to this wild mare whom he never fully understood. So he was operating from his instinct, the way it made sense to him to lead. While I felt so misunderstood, it turns out I had never understood him either. It wasn't until this moment that Robb made so much sense to me as I saw him through the mind, actions, and habits of our older son.

I spoke to Robb in my thoughts: *I get it now, honey. I get it.*

The boys and I licked our way through ice-cream cones at McDonald's, replaying the scene and talking about all the ways we had each contributed to our safety. When we ventured back home again, the snake was still there, still unmoving. I was now willing to consider the possibility that the snake was dead.

I would like to tell you that I swept in with superhuman courage and took care of the carcass, but I didn't. Later that afternoon my mom took care of the business. Seriously. Leave it to Grandma to come on over, bust out the shovel, and carry the dead snake into the woods.

Meanwhile, I stayed safely inside and considered my options related to the snake: either put the house on the market or have it demolished.

We have entered the season of the Lego. We were building a city bus. This was the goal. A forty-five-step process. We did forty-four of the steps. We realized too late one night (postbedtime) that we had forgotten to install the driver. And the passenger. Make that forty-three steps.

Too bad about the driver and passenger. We're not telling anybody.

This Lego City was Tyler's birthday present, but he couldn't do it on his own yet. Tucker and I put together the skateboard/bicycle shop, and Mom and Tyler began the city bus. But Tyler became more interested in attaching heads to bodies and buying a skateboard from the new shop owner.

So I moved over to help my mom at the bus factory.

Jobs were assigned: directions coordinators, parts distributors, and chief bus builder (me, naturally). Neither of us felt it necessary to remind the other that between us we did not have even one minute of past experience in building with Legos.

Tucker got carried away blowing headlights across the table. Tyler came in and out of the scene, depending on his interest and where we were in the process. His very favorite part was putting on wheels.

That was step forty-two. So he lingered.

As chief builder, I soon developed a vocabulary to shout across the table to the parts distributor.

"I need three black flatties."

"Black flatties?"

"Yes."

"How many?"

"Wait. More than three. Six."

"I only have five."

"Tuck, do you have a black flatty?"

"A black flatty? Or a black fatty?"

"A black flatty. Oh, wait—yes. And a black fatty."

"I need a rectangle triangle piece."

"Tricia, rectangle or triangle?"

"A rectangle triangle."

"Oh, you mean a sliding board." (Turns out my mom also has a vocabulary of her own.)

"Tuck, be careful with those headlights. We'll need them soon."

"Head lice? Who needs head lice?" pipes in my dad.

"Headlights, Dad. Headlights. And two yellow longies and a blue fatty."

"I have a blue skinny pants . . . Need that?"

Then I put two yellow flatties on top of two black flatties, only to realize they didn't match the directions. Oopsie daisy.

Mom has never been known for the strength of her fingernails, and I have never been known to use mine as pliers. So I handed them to Dad. 'Cause who has better fingernail tools than Dad?

He was at least willing. The first time.

He separated and returned my flatties. I put them back together, thinking I had been right all along, only to realize I was wrong about being right. "Hey, Dad? Can you take apart these long flatties?"

"Seriously?"

"Um, yes."

"If I do, would you not put them together again?"

"Sure." Except I did. Three more times. (Always sure I was right.)

"Tucker, the headlights. Please. Keep them close. This is no time to blow them off the table. We'll need them."

"Where's the blue longie? I need a blue longie. Blue longie. Blue longie. Anyone?"

Looking. Looking.

Tyler has it in his hot little hand. "I was saving it." *Right. Well, now's the moment for the big unveiling. Hand over the blue longie and nobody gets hurt.*

"Tuck, headlights, please."

"I only have one now, Mommy."

Right. Of course. They've been blown off the table.

Turns out, golden headlights match wood floors quite seamlessly.

Boys were under my elbows, dancing on chairs, blowing on headlights, and saving important pieces for future projects yet undesigned. In the end we had a city bus. Complete with windows, swinging doors (half with handles, half without), headlights, and five red seats. (No driver or passenger. See above.)

I handed it to Tyler, and he looked it over for quality control. "Hey, Mommy? This looks a little bit like a bus."

A little bit. Thank you, son.

Have you seen the movie *Ghost*? Patrick Swayze? Whoopi Goldberg? Demi Moore? I have thought of it many times. In the movie Sam sits near Molly in her daily life, watching her closely, even coaching from his invisible standpoint.

Now, I know Robb is in heaven; he's not the Patrick Swayze ghost in my life. Still, it was easy to imagine him in the empty chair across the table. I imagined him shaking his head, rolling his eyes at my Lego vocabulary, catching flying headlights, and saying, "Don't ask me to take 'em apart. I'm the one with fat fingers."

Just as Sam lifts the penny into the air to show Molly that he's there, I pictured Robb nudging the six-dotted red fatty across the table at just the right moment. I'm bummed he missed the Lego scene. It was pretty great. The wheels on the bus even turned, despite the absent driver.

fourteen

I have always been a "girlie girl," about as feminine as they come, with such poor depth perception that I have never in my life caught a ball, let alone hit one with a bat. And here I am, blessed with two little boys to raise.

I want to be a cool mom. I really do. I want to be the mom who brings fun snacks, who plays catch (even if she can't catch the football), who plays good music, and who can handle messy hands and grass-stained knees—if it means my sons had a good time getting that way. I want to be the cool mom who cheers appropriately at their events, the cool mom that my boys don't mind introducing to their friends, the cool mom who makes them laugh.

In fact, in my quiet efforts to be a cool mom, I actually spent some time in front of the bathroom mirror today practicing my really good explosion sound effects. (I'm not kidding. Yes, I happened to have my curling iron in hand, but that's beside the point.) I'm going to really impress them with that skill someday.

The boys and I began our Saturday morning by removing a hair clog from my bathtub. We're talking serious family fun, right there. I earned some significant points for the gross factor and my cartoonish monster sounds as it emerged. Buzz Lightyear even came to watch. Then he needed to spend the day on the couch to recover, Tyler explained.

The boys thought I was doing them some great favor by letting them watch. The truth is, they will be husbands someday. And it will be great if they enter marriage with the notion that this task is exceedingly cool.

However, I *do not* yet pass gas on command, and I have no intention of practicing or mastering that skill, no matter how cool it would make me. But I intend to make up for that weakness in other ways. I am coming to terms with the lost cause of eradicating rude words in our home. They're not totally inappropriate, just gross, annoying, and meaningless. You know the type: poop, peepee, butt, butthead . . . They roll off the tongue a little too easily. I'm making myself crazy with the constant badgering to eliminate such vocabulary, and it really is fruitless. I have two boys. They have an innate love for these words, for what will later be called locker-room humor. I am sorely outnumbered.

So here's the new rule for the boys: be respectful to ladies. There is primarily one girl in your life. She doesn't want to hear those words. If you must say them, then go outside or downstairs or in the bathroom or to the garage. But do not say them in the car, in my proximity, and most certainly not at my dinner table.

You are going to be gentlemen of respect, and I think we can start with this small request: don't make me listen to your garbage words. The policy is effective immediately. I will not change my mind. Take heed, young mosquitoes.

The school calendar is a conundrum to me. With all respect to those who work so hard to teach children, it really seems like we don't have more than nine consecutive days of school before it's time for another day off. For example, this is now fall break, which I think is poorly named and unnecessary. When I was growing up, fall break was called Thanksgiving.

We three fall-breakers started with Starbucks because who can't go for Starbucks in the morning? Well, clearly not me. And I'm raising a couple of baristas. I'm sure of it. An orange smoothie for him. A hot chocolate for him. An iced toffee nut Americano and a venti ice water for me. A collection of iPhone games for one boy, a barrage of educational websites on my laptop for the other, and I have found myself a bit of time to be quiet and read on my own. It's like a traveling DVD player in the car. Three cheers for parenting with technology. Hip, hip, hooray!

Tucker has a stain of chocolate around his lips. Tyler keeps kicking me under the table since his legs move with the characters on his screen. They're eating the leftovers from their lunchboxes. We are alone together. Together alone. Sharing space is a language.

The day was mostly a smashing success, except for the one or two hiccups that accompanied *every single thing* I planned.

We had lunch at a pizzeria. An order of breadsticks, a slice of pizza for each, a root beer for the tall boy, and an orange juice for the short one. Who doesn't love pizza and orange juice? A creative combination, undoubtedly. Except that having lunch alone with two small boys is really a romanticized idea that doesn't ever quite pan out like I think it will. I always picture conversation and memories. What I get instead is kicking and spills and jumping in the booth and peeking over the side and one boy finding gum under the table and the other boy putting it on his nose.

We did some wishful shopping at the toy store—the child's version of trying on an outfit you know you're not going to buy. Sometimes it's just good to tangibly enjoy the display.

We strolled to the movie theater to see what was playing that might get six thumbs up from our trio of reviewers. *Dolphin Tale* won out. Three tickets for the 3:05, please. And it would be great if you could seat us near people who don't mind the four-year-old's color commentary throughout. He likes to verbally replay everything that just happened and then ask a dozen questions about what he missed during his own instant replay. We're working on that. We bring the party with us, my friends. Or, perhaps they do. And I tag along for the adventure.

Another day in the same fall break (still poorly named), we visited the arcade with a handful of quarters for their glorious spending pleasure. Tuck spent his coins on experiences: virtual motorcycle rides and shooting galleries. Tyler spent his coins and best efforts on things: the claw game with sparkly, shiny promises inside.

Tuck found exactly what he was looking for; Tyler left empty handed. He was most distraught, begging for more quarters. It's a hard life lesson, that first trip to the arcade, when you realize the odds are against you and the machines are rigged.

"See, buddy, let me tell you: those are tricky machines, and it's very, very, very hard to win the things inside. But they don't want you to know that until you've put your quarters in and it's too late."

I did, by the way, warn him of this pitfall before he put his quarters in, before it was too late. But my words were useless until he experienced it for himself.

"Well, then that's a meany bully game."

"It is, kiddo. You're right."

"It tricked me."

"I know, buddy. That's how it happens sometimes."

You give what is asked, and you don't get what you want. The shiny promises leave you empty handed. He stationed himself outside the entrance of the arcade, personally alerting passersby to the fraud happening just inside those doors.

On our way out I gave each of them two more quarters to use in one of the guaranteed-prize vending machines. A hope for re-demption, albeit a toy no bigger than a dime. Tucker got a blue ninja. Score. Tyler got a green dinosaur. Disappointment struck again: it wasn't as big as the picture on the outside of the machine.

I get it, kiddo. I wish I could tell you that this isn't how it goes, that life owes you a full refund. Sometimes you have to invest your energy in listing all the ways you can imagine, pretend, and utilize a teeny-tiny green dinosaur.

Sometimes you just have to love what's in your hands.

My son wants to play baseball.

"Mommy, for my birthday I want a baseball and a bat and a mitt."

My eyes sting. *What is he going to do with a baseball? He doesn't have a partner to play with.*

A boy learns to play with the constant banter of throw and catch in the backyard. His dad teaches him to swing. His dad teaches him how to wear the mitt on one hand and secure the ball with the other.

His dad teaches him.

This little boy wants to play. And it's not that I don't want to be the one to teach him. It's that I can't. These jacked-up eyes do not assist in catching a ball, hitting with a bat, lighting a candle, cutting a string, or painting my toenails. Any of the above can happen by accident but not usually without incident.

But my son wants to play ball. Baseball, please.

A fellow parent solved this one for me. "Oh, this is an easy one. Get him a T-ball with a string so he can hit the ball as hard as he wants and it will always come back. As for catching and throwing, get him a pitching net. He can throw and catch for hours, all on his own."

And so I will. Because I am up for an easy fix for any one of these sneak attacks.

And because my boy wants to play ball.

And I can't be his dad.

If ever there is an epic battle of wills, it is to teach a boy to ride a bike when he does not want to learn. And yet there are things you have to learn when you are less than four feet tall, because it only gets harder and the courage only fades as one gets taller. And so this was the weekend. The milestone that would forever define before and after.

The good news is that I took off the training wheels by my very own self. The less good news is that we had to go to the bike shop to finish the job.

I let him pick the park where he would metaphorically army crawl through the trenches.

There was cheering and clapping.

There was throwing of helmets.

There was encouragement and bribery.

There were pictures and videos.

There were tears and drama.

How do you know when to push your kids further and when to let them give up?

I may or may not have said things like "You will get on this bike, you will pedal and keep your balance, and you will like it."

And finally, "Buddy, if you will try one more time, I will pay you twenty dollars. Twenty bucks. Cold, hard cash."

I'm just saying, the kid can ride a bike now.

Someday I believe he will thank me for making him do what I really wanted him to learn to do.

I said, "You were awesome."

He glared and said, "You. Were not."

At the park a little boy was zooming along the sidewalk, hit a crack or a twig or a toy or something else, and did an aerial flip over the handles of his scooter, head over heels. Not my son. This time it was someone else's little boy.

There was an audible gasp among the collective parents. Several came running, helped him to his feet, and gave him the once-over. I scrambled in my bag. "Band-Aids. I have Band-Aids." It was a community effort.

Screaming, the boy took one look at all of us, and he tried to part the waters to find his mom.

"Mom! Mom! I need my mom!"

She appeared then, and he breathed easier once he saw her. At that age breathing easier means crying more freely. He cried and cried.

The spectating parents gave her the details.

"He was going so fast . . ."

"He was really scootin' along!"

"He ran over something, and he just flew right over the handlebars . . ."

"Good thing for that helmet, eh?"

She looked sheepishly at the team of reporters, her eyes offering a silent explanation: *I'm not a bad mom. I just didn't see it happen. I just didn't see it.*

Oh, I get that. Fear not, nameless friend. It could have just as easily been my child, my easy distraction, my sense of guilt for not catching or at least watching his fall.

In fact, last week it was my child. *Sarcasm alert:* I gave myself extra points on the tally for Mom of the Year when a stranger at the pool had to tell me my son was standing by the ladder crying after he hit his head coming down the slide.

Nothing feels better than when somebody else nurtures your

child because you simply weren't paying attention. That's *awesome*. Not.

It's a full-time job. And even if you never take your eyes off them, they're still going to fall.

It's what you do next that matters.

Part Five

whole all along

W e were driving home in the still of a spring night, and we drove past the park where we have spent so many of our afternoons. I heard his voice from the backseat, my older son who so often airs his thoughts in the car.

"The lights are out at the park. Nobody is playing there."

"Yes, that's because it's nighttime and the park closes when the sun goes down. Did you know that?"

"Yes, and what happens if someone still goes to the park when it's closed?"

"Well, a policeman could come and ask him to leave, or the policeman might ask him to pay some money because he broke the rule."

"Like three hundred dollars?"

"Maybe. Or like one hundred dollars. Or something." I don't really know the fine for trespassing after dusk.

"Does everyone know the laws around here?"

"I think so." If not, people'll know when they break one. Or when they get caught. But for the purposes of this late-night conversation, let's assume everyone knows the rules. Still, the question about people breaking laws at night sparks Tyler to join the conversation as well.

"Mommy," Tyler asks, "if someone sneaks into our bedroom,

if we hear them stomp up the stairs, then we should pretend we are asleep, right?"

I want to tell them both that nothing like this would ever happen. But then I remember a friend from my childhood, Rachel, who was awake when someone robbed her home, and she knew what to do because her mother had told her to lie very still in the case of such an emergency.

"Yes, be very still. Pretend you are sleeping. But remember: we have a security system, so the police would know we needed them, and they would come right away."

"Would they go one hundred?" Tucker asks.

"I don't really know what that means."

"Would they go one hundred?"

Still, I'm not clear. And then I glance at my speedometer and see three letters: MPH. "Oh, one hundred miles per hour? Yes, buddy. I'm sure they would."

"Mommy, do you remember when the police came?" Tucker continues.

"Yes, I remember."

"And you carried me really quickly out to Miss Melody's car."

"I sure did."

"You carried me out because you wanted to see Daddy dead all by yourself."

We haven't talked about this in a long time. His vocabulary has changed since we last remembered together.

"Well, I carried you out to Miss Melody because I knew Daddy had died, and I had a lot of decisions to make. And I wanted you to be able to play and be happy for one more day before everything would change for you."

"You cried a lot that day, Mommy."

"I did."

"Sometimes you still need to cry for Daddy."

"Sometimes I do. I cried for him today." *I'll tell you why another day.*

"But tomorrow is a new day, Mommy. That's what Chicken Little says."

Yes. So does Scarlett O'Hara.

"Mommy, we need a new daddy."

"We do. We will have him when it's time."

"You need him the most, Mommy. You need to stop crying."

"It won't be the new daddy's job to help me stop crying, but it will be wonderful when he is part of us."

"How old is our country?"

Quick math while I'm driving . . . Take away 1776 from 2015. "Um, I think about 240 years." (I know it's not right. It was an estimate.)

"So on the country's next birthday, it will turn 241?"

"I'm not really sure." I'm content to let him think I don't know what I'm talking about. I do know how to do four-digit subtraction in my head, but I'm not doing it right now.

"How many dollars are in three million pennies?"

And now I'm mentally moving the decimal point two spaces. "Um, let's see. Three thousand dollars. Or maybe thirty thousand. We can figure it out tomorrow." I can't seem to count zeroes in my head, especially not while I'm pulling the car into the garage.

I park the car and help them out of their car seats as the questions continue. "Do all the people in the world like all the people in the world?"

Topics shift as quickly as *Sesame Street* segments around here, and suddenly we are discussing world peace. "Well, not everybody likes everybody. But it would be great if they did."

"But the people who have the devil in their hearts—do they like everyone?"

"I don't really know." Someday he will see that even people who have Jesus in their hearts don't always like everyone.

"Can I have dessert?"

"Just two. There are some in the Tupperware on the counter."

While Tucker navigates the Tupperware seal, Tyler stands in front of the open refrigerator with a cup in his hand. "Mommy," he says with a puckered face, "I tried this juice, and I just really don't like it."

"Well, that's because you poured yourself eight ounces of homemade salad dressing."

"Oh. Can I have juice?"

"You may have water or milk."

"I want juice."

"You may have water or milk."

"Can you get it?"

"I will show you how, and you may forevermore do it yourself."

He opts for water, and he pours a glass for his brother just for the sheer joy of using the water dispenser. We walk up the stairs with water cups in hand.

"Can you read us a story?" the taller one asks.

"Not tonight, lovey."

"You never do," the shorter one mutters.

"That's not true at all, and it's not fair for you to say *never*."

"Well, you don't read the ones I like. You only read grown-up books to us."

"That's bunk. *Junie B. Jones* is open on your nightstand."

"I want you to read a chapter tonight."

"I'm exhausted, buddy. I can't read anything aloud tonight. Plus, tomorrow we're getting like eighty-seven inches of snow, so I'll read to you tomorrow—as many books as you want, whichever ones you like the most."

Pouty face.

Whatever. I've got so many other things to worry about; pouting doesn't even make the radar around here.

Kisses. Hugs. Prayers.

"I'm sorry I was impatient today, guys. Please forgive me."

"I forgive you."

"Me too, Mommy."

They echo each other, and I think to myself, *It would be nice if you asked forgiveness for not listening well, but tonight I'll model humility and not scorekeeping.*

On my way out I trip over Buzz Lightyear, who instantly and automatically declares an intergalactic emergency. *Buzz, call it a night. We are two hours past bedtime, and you are not helping.*

I make myself a Keurig cup of decaf coffee with mocha creamer, light a pumpkin-scented candle, grab a fleece blanket, and fold my legs under me in the corner of the sectional couch where my book lies facedown and open from last night. Tucker hops down the stairs like a merman, both of his legs in one pant leg. He says Tyler made him do it. Tyler shows up right behind him as I hear myself say everybody is in charge of his own pants. Everybody, get up the stairs. There is arguing and refusal. There is weeping and gnashing of teeth. There are empty threats and bribery.

If you knew how much I've done for you today, you wouldn't use that tone with me. Take your tone to bed.

Sometimes I wish there was someone else for them to call for. "Mommy. Mommy. Mommy." Incessant.

Except one of them says it so quickly that it comes out, "My. My. My." And the two seem to mean the same thing. I'm spent tonight. Poured out. Nothing left, guys.

This night I'd like to climb into someone's arms. Not just anyone's, though. It wouldn't be his job to make me happy or less tired, but it would be nice to have him here. It would be nice to feel safe. And held. And part of a team.

It's hard to demand respect without a model to show what it looks like. And there's something about a dad's voice. Just something.

There's a voice I miss:

"Listen to your mother."

"Don't talk to your mom that way."

"Don't ask her why. Just obey her. Because I'm your dad, and she's my wife."

I miss the tag team. Big time.

sixteen

Dallas to Denver. Seat 23B. It's in the middle. I sit between two men, one young, one old. (Young = high school. Old = retired—at least in this story.)

The man sitting across the aisle seems like he could turn his head my way and be my husband. Not that I've fallen in love with the man across the aisle, but from this angle, with my reading glasses on so my distance vision is a little blurred, he looks like Robb.

It's an interesting encounter because I have spent a fair amount of energy being mad at Robb recently. Admittedly, I still get mad at him for silly little things, and the little things add up to become one great big chasm between two people.

I just went through security at the airport, and I took my time. I am not efficient, but I make up for it with a winsome and cheerful personality. Robb valued efficiency above all else, so I always annoyed him when we went through the security line at the airport. I was never quite ready to take my shoes off, put my shoes on, move forward, or step back—whatever was the next dance move. I didn't move quickly enough.

With Robb it was a fatal error not to check in online for the flight at our earliest opportunity. Especially because Southwest has no assigned seating, and of course we would want premier choices in seating. (He was always on the aisle; I was always in the middle. Always.)

Okay, not always. There were times when we flew with the boys, and he sat with them while I sat across the aisle with the strangers. Robb put in a movie for our children, they had the space and time they needed on their boys' side of the plane, and I settled in with my good book.

You know what I did today? I was so careless and irresponsible that I didn't check in before I arrived at the airport. I left it all to chance and checked in at the "check-in counter." Which they have for people like me.

And when it was time to board the flight, I didn't jump to attention and stand near the door, waiting to board immediately and as quickly as possible. I let other people go in front of me. I finished my banana smoothie. I didn't care if I was the last one on the plane. How bad could it be? I spent an entire marriage sitting in the middle seat, so it's very familiar and homey to me.

I was such a rebel today. I went through the airport at my leisure, doing everything the way I wanted to, slowly and with a friendly spirit. And I made the flight on time, and I have a seat that is just fine, thank you.

So my spirit stirs with freedom, remembering all his little quirks that grated on me. *Hey, Robb? I broke all your rules today, and nothing bad happened. Like, nothing bad at all.*

But now I'm sitting near this man who has Robb's broad shoulders and his neck and wears his business suit the very same way Robb did. And I look at him, and I soften.

I imagine what it would be like if he turned to me, if he were

Robb, if I could talk to him. And I think about what that conversation would be like, how gentle and kind. And I remember that he loved me so fiercely, and he took care of me with great pride and intentionality. He wasn't trying to stifle my spirit; it's just that he felt as if he were holding the reins of a wild mare sometimes. And somehow he needed to get us on the plane.

I look at this kind, gentle stranger whose lines look like Robb's, and I forgive my husband all over again. And that's how it was when Robb was here.

I could be so spun up, so worn out with little misunderstandings that were causing serious miscommunications. But then I would catch a glimpse of him. He might have been working at his computer, his eyes doing that careful squint. He might have been watching TV. His favorites were anything animated, and he was perpetually smiling when cartoons were on the screen. I would look at him, and I would see the soft lines of the smooth-faced boy I fell in love with. And I would soften and forgive him.

My reverie is interrupted by the young man sitting directly beside me. He looks as if he's younger than twenty, and he's wearing a college T-shirt and a baseball cap, both frayed and worn but probably new since we now pay for clothes to look damaged instead of keeping them long enough to wear them out ourselves. The young man gazes out his window, looking back at the airport. "It's depressing to leave my family," he mutters.

I don't talk much to strangers anymore, but this was a sentence I could acknowledge. "Oh, I'm sorry. Yes, I bet it is."

"My family lives in Texas, but I go to school in Colorado. Are you from Texas?"

"No, I'm from Denver."

"Oh. 'Cause you sound like you're from Texas." I had handed him eight words. And in them he found a Texas accent. I raise my eyebrows in response, not really sure what else to say. In another season I might have fluttered with paragraphs about where I'm originally from, how interesting accents are, the salad bowl of the United States—really, any number of topics. I simply raise my eyebrows. Nod slightly. I don't really have a response other than that, but he is finished with his observation anyway. Back to his longing looks out the window. Once we reach prime elevation, I break out the laptop. Type, type, type. Click, click, click.

"So, is that like some summary or something you're writing for a class?" asks the young man. He has been reading over my shoulder. I can't say I haven't done the same thing. There isn't much privacy in the forced intimacy of coach on plane flights.

"Oh, no, I'm working on a manuscript."

"Dude. You're a writer?"

"I am."

"Oh. That's weird. I hate books."

I raise my eyebrows. Nod slightly. *I'm glad we had this talk,* I think.

"We'll need you to power down now, ma'am," says the airline attendant, gathering one last round of trash. I shut down the laptop and exchange it for my current paperback, another from the collections of Madeleine L'Engle. Man, I love her.

The older man speaks from the other side. "So, as a writer, don't you worry about reading other people's stuff? Like you might plagiarize it or something?"

This is our opening dialogue, at the end of the flight. We hadn't exchanged words yet, although I had retrieved several things for him from the floor between our seats since he doesn't have a left arm and kept dropping things.

"Well, I'm pretty careful."

"My goodness, if I were a writer, I'd never read anybody else's book ever again. All I'd do is write so I could make sure it was my own stuff. I mean, don't you ever write something and then think, 'Wait, did I think of that, or did it come from somebody else, something else I read?'"

In another season I might have launched into a diatribe about the benefits of a writer's reading, about building one's thoughts on the inspiration of others, about the truth that good writers are good readers. Instead, I say, "Well, I've always got a few books going at once, so I guess there are always a few voices speaking into my writing."

"Do you write for children?"

"No, mostly adults." Which is a better response than when I accidentally told a roofer that I write adult novels.

"What do you write about?"

I should say "A public journal of the perils of dog walking." But I'm not quick enough on the draw. I am honest instead. "I am recently widowed. I'm writing about this first year without my husband."

"Ah. And what did your husband do?" Not typically the first response, but I'll roll with it.

"He was a corporate trainer for a national insurance company. Farmers Insurance, actually."

"Oh, so he probably knows that actor who does the Farmers commercials about their specialized training."

Wow. Um, just, wow. "Well, no, he didn't know the actor, but he was on the team that wrote that curriculum."

The man elbows me with his half arm. "I'm just kiddin' with ya. Just joshin'. You know, that actor? He used to play the psychologist on one of those lawyer shows, and he has always played such a smart guy until he played that one role in a movie with Tom Hanks. I'll tell ya, in that movie he played such an idiot, a real know-it-all. Blew off his own dog's face."

Oh. My word. I open my book. Madeleine is so much safer than this. (Robb would say, "Tricia, this is what you get for talking to the person next to you. Just keep your headphones on. That's what I always do.")

This guy pays no attention to my nonverbal cues. He plods ahead. "You know, the bottom line is whether they sell more insurance."

Is that really the bottom line? Really?

"You know, I'm old enough to remember the old beer commercials with sophisticated humor, and those commercials were a really big hit. But the problem is that the people with sophisticated humor weren't the ones buying all the beer, so really their ad campaign didn't work at all. The bottom line is whether they sell more of their product."

"Yes, I guess it is." I open my book. I put on my headphones, even though the FAA prohibits the use of all electronics during takeoff and landing. Madeleine and I cruise together to a safe landing, between these two oddballs. I'm taking her with me everywhere.

I make it home and snuggle with my sweet boys on the couch, a tangle of arms and legs. And shoelaces.

"Mommy, I wish you weren't an author."

"Why, lovey?"

"Because I don't want you to teach other places and be gone and travel to all these other countries."

I try to remind them of our many evenings at home, our late-night snacks, our movie nights. I try to remind them that we had a great trio date a few nights ago, complete with extra cheese on our pizza. I try to explain that this is my job now, this author gig. I think about explaining words like *mortgage*. I try to tell them that I'm obeying God by teaching and writing the words he has given me. But none of these things matters to them. And too much of "God's will" could just make them resent God for keeping their mom's calendar full.

I let them talk and cry and grapple with shoelaces until I realize this cycle is going nowhere good. It's after nine o'clock, and we have in our genetic composition a curfew on rationality. Stay up too late, and we're toast. Sleep is the only cure.

"Mommy, maybe you can write a poem for us. So when you die, and Grandma and Poppa own us, then they could read it to us."

Nothing I ever say seems to make them believe I am safe, here, and not secretly dying.

I carry them to their bedroom. "Boys, let me tell you a bedtime story. It's about two boys, and their names are Toby and Tanner."

"They start with *T*, just like us!"

"Are there sisters in the story? There should be sisters. Taylor . . . and Twister."

"Twister is a boy's name."

"Then she could be called Rosie. Toby, Tanner, Taylor, and Rosie."

"I want them to be called Tucker and Tyler. And Tricia."

"Oh, like us?"

"Yes. Us."

"Which one are you?"

"I'll be Tucker."

"And I'll be Tyler."

Deal. I'll be Tricia, and this story is getting much easier to tell.

"Once upon a time, there was a mommy and two little boys. And the mommy became an author. She wrote books, and people read them. And sometimes the people wanted her to read to them, or talk to them, or teach them. So the mommy, Tricia, obeyed God, and she shared all the words he had given her. And sometimes that meant she was gone for an evening or a day or a night or two."

"Or four." *Right. That upcoming trip to the country of Ohio will be for four days.*

"But no matter how many books she wrote, no matter what people called her—writer, author, speaker, teacher—the most important name was the first one she had been given: Mommy. She loved her children more than anything in the world."

"More than God?"

"Well, she loved them differently than God. God made her, so she worshiped him. And God gave her these two boys, so she worshiped him. But she loved these boys more than anyone else in the world."

My boys study my face, looking for truths in the twin bed we're sharing.

"The mommy traveled sometimes, but she always came back. And they could call her anytime they wanted to, and they could do FaceTime, and she left them gifts to open every single day."

"Did she mail them?"

"No, she prepared them before she left." (And now she's adding this to her list of tasks before traveling next week.)

"She always came back, she was always there when they needed her, but they did not always need her. They were smart, safe boys, and their mom loved them the most."

Someone tooted in that tender moment, which was just the tension breaker we needed. And my cue to wrap things up.

I kissed them each, hugged them tight. "Good night, my loves. I love you more than all the books in the world."

I stepped into the darkness of the hallway. I blew them one more kiss that they'll never see.

God, help me to do this well.

You know I love my sweet boys. You know I do. And I think we are in a good place, thus far my favorite season of parenting, this age when they can tie their own shoes, pack their lunches, and, most important, make me laugh. But let me say, there have been many seasons when I have often wondered if I might lose my parenting license over potty training or the child who is learning to scowl and shout his opinions. There have been ragged moments when I wanted to look at them and say, "Do you know that I wasn't always like this? Do you know that I'm smart? Do you know that I'm bigger than this lifestyle we share? Are either of you thankful for how many times I read that silly book to you? What about the Play-Doh whose scent has permanently seeped into my hands? What about the disintegrated diaper in the wash and the stale french fries in the car? Do you know that I have a degree and aspirations that are so much bigger than laundry and diapers? Do you know that I love you and adore you and cannot imagine my life without you, but this day is breaking me?"

There are miracles every day, but I often climb into bed wondering, *Was today miraculous? Even slightly? It sure didn't feel like it . . . It felt small. Very small.* I dream big. Bigger than this. And so I remind God of all the things I want, of the lifetime goals that seem to lie on a path separate from mine, of the things I want to do with my mind and my skills. Just in case he forgot, I give him my list. And in his faithfulness, in ways beyond measure, words, or understanding, he restores my soul. He quiets my heart, he refreshes me with love, and he gives me rest.

At the end of the day, that's what I need: precious sleep.

I am reading Sandra Aldrich's book *From One Single Mother to Another.* She too was widowed with small children, and she wrote a book—decades ago now—encouraging the rest of us who follow in the footsteps of her journey.

Sandra wrote, "As I entered my second year of singlehood, well-meaning friends asked me when I'd get married again. I laughingly answered I wouldn't even think about that until somebody showed up with a dozen roses. Then I changed the subject."

This pat answer drove her to a place of asking a deeper question: "Would I really be attracted to the first guy who handed me roses?" Sandra admitted to herself that he would indeed get her attention, but she made an important decision instead: She would plant her own garden. Physically.

She went to the local gardening shop and loaded the trunk of her car with rosebushes and bags of peat moss. For the next many months, she nurtured fresh roses and marveled at the beauty and satisfaction of fresh, fragrant blooms in her home.

And she didn't even need a man to bring them to her.

As I read about how Sandra began to "plant her own garden" in other areas of her life as well, I thought about my own "garden" I've been creating. A new home. A new career of writing, speaking, and teaching. I bought myself an emerald ring—physical evidence on my hand that life has indeed come back. I am okay. Green means life and growth. And I didn't need a man to make the decision or the purchase for me.

"I think every girl should buy herself a ring." My friend Sunny told me that her grandmother had told her this. Sunny's grandma had been married for twenty-five years when her husband left, and as she re-created her life, she bought herself a ring. It's a piece that almost always represents a commitment, and it's almost always a gift. So she bought one for herself, believing herself worthy of such a gift and committing to her own health and wellness and satisfaction. And she believed every girl should do the same thing at some point in her life.

Just to clarify, I haven't become a raging bra-burning feminist who is out to set the world free from marriage. I still very much love the institution of marriage, and I would very much love to be married once again. I'm not making any promises to remain forever single. My goodness, I'd love to do it all again.

But I can't deny the strength I have found in remaining single, in choosing to learn who I am. I have been Doyle and Polly's daughter, Rob's sister, Robb's wife, Tucker and Tyler's mom. If I hadn't taken this time to get to know me—the Tricia when nobody else is around—I wouldn't have found this strong, courageous woman. I wouldn't have known that my favorite color is really grass green. I wouldn't have learned that I like mushrooms, because I never had a reason to prepare them. I wouldn't have known how to haggle over financing for a car and how to negotiate the down payment for a house. I wouldn't have known how I really, truly feel about silly little things like wall color (rich, deep earth tones) and fabric softener (the best thing about laundry) and throw pillows (there's always room for more), because I was in a very comfortable pattern of deferring to someone else's preferences.

It's good for a girl to learn the sound of her own voice.

seventeen

Robb and I went on a whitewater rafting trip when we had been married for a year or so. We camped with probably a dozen other couples, and we all donned our lifejackets and hit the rapids the next day.

I remember feeling that combination of fear and excitement and incredulity and bravery and *what are we thinking* but being so ready to do this because it was on our collective bucket list.

We listened carefully to the guide, concentrating on his advice on how to handle the greatest risk.

"If you get knocked out of the boat, don't try to fight the current. Don't try to stand, swim against the current, or even swim to a bank on the side. Just pick up your knees and let the water carry you. It's stronger than you, bigger than you, and it's going to do what it's going to do. If you fight it, you're only wasting your energy and causing a greater risk to yourself. So pick up your knees, float on your back, and wait to see where the river takes you. It's the safest thing you can do, and I promise we will come find you wherever you land."

I don't recall that I needed to heed his advice, particularly because the water level was at a record low that summer, and at one point we actually got out of the raft and carried it across the exposed rocks in the middle of the river.

But his words found their way into my subconscious, surfacing many years later on an August morning when Robb would have turned thirty-six. I went to sleep the eve before with the full knowledge that the following morning was Robb's birthday. But when I woke up, I didn't remember until I felt so burdened I could barely move, buried underneath an invisible reminder. I traced the lethargy. *Why do I feel so horrible today? Why do I want to skip the next twenty-four hours? What is happening today that I'm dreading, dreading, dreading?* When a date is etched into my mind, my subconscious will always be aware when the date arrives yet again. It will whisper to me in dry, gray tones until I finally read the memo.

And then it hit me with gale force, nearly sending me straight back to bed. Except that I had two little boys to whom I had promised doughnuts for breakfast. I had doled out that promise when my heart was lighter with the promise of traditions. I followed through with the doughnuts, but it's all the celebration I had in me.

I could not celebrate, would not celebrate. I resisted every "should" that came to my mind. And I will resist yours too if you tell me right now how I could have honored my husband better or differently.

I remembered him all day.

I remembered the six years in a row that I ruined his birthday cake. Six years in a row. (Birthday cakes are just not my gig. Although I aspire to dreams of *Cupcake Wars* and *Food Network Challenge,* it's all a big farce.)

I remembered breakfasts in bed and runaway days and surprising him with doughnuts at the office and teaching little boys to celebrate and struggling to find the perfect gift for a man who really wanted nothing at all. I remembered his birthday the last year before he died, when we planned an impromptu out-of-town excursion for the four of us, complete with a hotel pool, late-night movies, jumping on the bed, and barbecue pulled pork, although not all of those together in the same scene.

I remembered him all day.

It is insanely impossible to celebrate the birthday of someone who was recently stolen from me. It's like buying baby clothes after the miscarriage has been confirmed; it cannot be done without a high degree of lying to yourself. On his birthday, a day that I have forever cherished, I let it pass me by, one hour at a time. This was perhaps the hardest milestone yet. I climbed back into bed, feeling like a failure for not pushing through and getting myself out of bed and out of the house. *I'll just sleep for an hour,* I told myself. *Just for an hour. Or two.* Or just a little bit longer.

I slept until three that afternoon.

Just as the guide had said, when you're knocked out of the boat, don't fight what is stronger than you. Lift your knees, surrender to the current, and let it carry you until it sets you down.

At three o'clock, after sleeping the very day away, I was very suddenly just finished. I needed to shift the tone of the day. I got dressed, including boots and a great pashmina. I smiled at my dolled-up self in the mirror as I put on a smooth layer of lip gloss.

I am changing. This is aging me, I thought. *My spirit is becoming older. My face isn't as young. My eyes crinkle like crepe paper. I seem too young to feel so old. And I don't even care. It was bound to happen sometime. I'd rather give my youth to a broken*

heart than hand it over to sun damage. Bring it on, wrinkles. Tell
my story. Age me well.

It's crazy how the pendulum swings, and all bets are off on
days of remembering. My impulsive nature hit with full force, I felt
compelled to make a memory, and I was ready to do something
fun. The boys had two days off from school during the long weekend of Robb's birthday, so I signed on to Priceline to book a last-
minute adventure. I firmly believe that Priceline was designed for
the adventurous spirit who wants to get away fast, *now,* and the
where doesn't matter. Still, the prize of rolling the dice with Priceline is sometimes golden and sometimes stained copper. This
brought us to a hotel that I would learn was one part *The Shining*
and one part Grandma's TV room. Stale cigarette smell included.

As we checked in, Tyler slipped away to a phone in the lobby,
and he called the front desk. "Excuse me," said Cindy, the big-
haired lady, as she dismissed herself from my transaction to answer the phone. (Sorry. That's my son calling you. Pay no attention,
please. He has no familiarity with corded phones.) That's a grand
start.

I got them to the pool as quickly as possible, and I set them
free to swim and splash. My children perfected running cannon-
balls into the hot tub and then rescued each other with the life
preserver. That continued until Tuck got so tangled in the rope
that the life preserver seemed to threaten the very opposite.

We transitioned to dinner and chose a nearby pizza joint. On
our getaway night, as we ate greasy pizza under a neon light, and
they played iPod games and I read a book, the whole scene disin-

tegrated in my mind. It was suddenly sad and lonely and pathetic and not at all fun.

The hotel scene didn't improve when we got back after dinner. It was ever-so-appallingly only 7:15, and we were in those weird hours of the night when it's hard to find wholesome TV for kids. The boys spread out on the pullout couch to watch some of their old favorites on those upper cable channels, like *Thomas & Friends* and *Angelina Ballerina*. I was in part charmed that these benign options still interest them and in part annoyed with the Cartoon Network for acting as if anything animated is appropriate for children.

I was in a big bed by myself, which is oddly better than being sandwiched between my sons, the two creeping crawlers with a dozen knees and elbows, and that's when it occurred to me: on the weekend of my dead husband's birthday, no amount of adventure can outrun lonely.

I would have packed us up and gone home—and believe you me, I wanted to—but the boys were ensnared with the pullout couch and the Sprout *Good Night Show*, and I couldn't let myself become the mom who breaks a promise.

Instead of bailing I called for reinforcements. And companionship. And snacks.

Text: *Mom, this is not fun. Could you come? Please bring fun. And snacks.*

And that's when I was deeply thankful we had chosen a hotel fifteen minutes from home for this ridiculous adventure. Within an hour my mom appeared with all her pixie dust and optimism and conversation and friendship. She brought Pop-Tarts, white cheddar Cheez-Its, M&M's, chocolate muffins, bottled water, Pringles, Mounds, and Diet Pepsi. She saved the night. Suddenly we were a veritable slumber party.

What did I learn?

a. No amount of planning and running and going can quiet the whispering threats of old memories on the calendar.

b. An adventure with my kids can still feel like a challenge of my own.

c. Everything's better when you bring a friend along.

d. And never underestimate the importance of late-night snacks in a hotel room.

At the end of it all, one of the boys said, "This was the best weekend ever. Because Mommy went to the bathroom once with the door open."

Really? That was the highlight? Honestly. I could have done that at home.

Anyway, we celebrated, and then it was over. I've never been so eager to watch the calendar pages fly, and never have I been so desperate to simultaneously make them all stop their blessed turning.

I finished the weekend with a mental love note.

Happy birthday to you, Robb. August 27 will never, ever— never, ever in my life—be the same.

The worst part of the big dates on the calendar—anniversaries, birthdays, days we shared, days everyone still shares in capital letters on their calendar—is the anticipation.

It's the pattern. And I know it's the pattern. But when I'm in it, it hardly matters that it's a predictable pattern. All that seems true is that I'm swimming in dread and remembering, and anxiety squeezes my entire body like a blood-pressure cuff until I can't stand it one more minute, and I'll do anything—anything—to make this stop.

Our wedding anniversary falls two days before my birthday, and there was a point in that week when the messages of "I'll do anything to make this end" were louder and more powerful than the messages of "This is part of the pattern, and tomorrow will be better and easier. You are okay." If there had been alcohol in the house, I would have drunk it all. If there had been mind-altering drugs, I would have taken them by the handful. Consequences be hanged. *Just let me end this. Let me stop feeling.* I was terrified of myself.

My crisis team surrounded me, in body and on the phone. If I said the magic words, we would be off to the hospital. If my therapist knew we were past the point of management, we were off to the hospital. I didn't have the courage to say it myself, but I would have let them take me anywhere.

In my bed weeping, I called my therapist. I listened to Jana's voice on the phone.

"Tricia, you are okay."

"I am not okay."

"Listen to me. You are okay. Your mind is wound around all the things that this week represents, with your birthday and your anniversary and a dozen other smaller things. Your mind is begging you to stop thinking. Your number-one job right now is to go to sleep. I want you to take your sleeping pill and lie very still, and whenever anything comes into your mind, you can tell it, 'Not now. I'm not thinking about this right now. I'm going to sleep.'"

"I'm going to sleep. I'm going to sleep." I practiced the mantra.

"That's right," Jana said. "Just like that. Right to sleep. Call me in the morning, or you know I'm going to harass you with phone calls and texts until I know where you are and how you are."

She's not kidding. I love this about her. There could be no better therapist anywhere, no one more suited to me.

"I'm going to sleep. I'm going to sleep." I laid the phone next to me on the bed and closed my eyes.

"Mommy? Are you crying?" Tyler stood in my doorway.

"Yes, baby. I'm crying." I'm crying a lot. A lot.

Tyler is a fixer and a gifter. He is compelled to bring me things that might help the problem at hand. He brought me tissues. He brought me the Cinderella doll. "Here, Mommy. Here." He piled things around me, trying to build a comforting nest.

"Here, Mommy. Look at this." I opened my eyes to see the picture he had drawn and framed himself (he took a different picture out of the frame by my bedside and replaced it with this one). It's a picture of our family of four, and we are all a bunch of floating heads. The boys and I are clustered together, and a couple of inches away toward the upper right is Robb. He's portrayed with a good measure of black. "Here, Mommy. I made this. Look."

"I can't look at that right now, lovey."

"I'll be right back."

He came back with a bound picture book I had made for him. Quite appropriately it is titled *Tyler and Daddy*. "Here, Mommy. Look at this. When you miss Daddy, you should look at this."

"No. No. No, Tyler. I cannot. I can't." I felt the panic rising again, and I was afraid I might lose myself and yell at him. I was supposed to be falling asleep. That was the plan.

He climbed onto my bed and sprawled himself across me, his head resting on my heart. "Hey, Mommy?"

"Yes, buddy?"

"Do you remember the night when Daddy died?"

"Yes, I do."

"Do you remember when you needed to give him medicine, and you asked me to go away?"

I do not clearly remember this, but I can picture it. I probably needed to give Robb some dosage of something, and at the same time three-year-old Tyler was trying to climb into the recliner and into the middle of everything. I'm sure I said something like, "Tyler, not now. Please be somewhere else." And this is what he remembers. On the day that Daddy died, I asked him to go away.

"Mommy, I watched and I watched. I stared and stared. And do you know why? It's because I wanted to see what someone looks like when they die."

It doesn't matter that in this story, the part he remembers, we had no idea that death was imminent. His memory is his reality.

"And now I know what happens. They just—poof!" His hands modeled a small explosion of pixie dust.

"No, baby. That's not what happens."

"Oh, I mean the person becomes invisible."

"No, that's not what happens either."

"Well, what happens?"

I am supposed to be sleeping. That's what Jana said. But there is a six-year-old in my arms, listening to my voice through the muffled, echoed caverns of my chest.

"His spirit left his body. But his body stayed."

"Then where is his body?"

"The doctors took it."

"Well, I want it."

"No, you don't, sugar. You think you do, and I know how that feels. But you don't want his body. It's not how you remember him. His body is empty now. His spirit is what we loved most, and his spirit is in heaven with Jesus."

"Oh. Well, I want his body. I want him."

"Me too."

And suddenly I realized that this is another moment he will take with him. He remembers that fleeting moment when I asked him to walk away, and he was only three. Now he is six, and memories have more cognitive space to take root. He will remember this night, his mommy and her puffy eyes, her frantic voice that became softer and softer as the sleeping pill took effect. He will remember how he tried to help. He will remember that I had no answers that were good enough. He will remember this.

I breathed deeply. I stroked his hair. "Tyler, do you know you're the happiest thing in my life?"

He lifted his head to look at me. "What? No, I didn't know that."

"Oh, sweet boy. You are. You are the happiest thing in my life. You're the reason I am alive, buddy."

His smile consumed us both. "The very happiest thing?"

"The very happiest thing."

Dear God, let this be what he remembers of this horrible night on the edge of my existence.

eighteen

Robb and I went on probably a thousand dates in the course of our marriage. But when I look back over the whole of them, it's not necessarily the most elaborate ones that win the sparkly award of remembering. Some of my favorites emerge from experiences that weren't really "dates" at all—when we were fixing dinner together, folding laundry, planting petunias, sorting baby clothes, taking a walk around the neighborhood, or grabbing a hot dog and chips at the cart outside Home Depot.

Now, believe you me, we had some s-t-e-l-l-a-r dates. But they didn't come out of nowhere. They were born of a life together. They were born of a lot of days and meals and errands and chores. If you live a lot of life, then some amazing, glittery, sparkling moments will rise to the top. Quantity is the gateway to quality.

We had a no-good, very bad, terrible, horrible history of watching movies together. Any trip to Blockbuster ended in an argument and extreme conclusions drawn about ourselves and our marriage. Robb had lots of criteria for a movie: If it didn't have enough big names in it, then it probably was a terrible movie because they couldn't interest any good actors to be in a terrible movie. If it had too many big names in it, then he assumed they had to invest in so many good actors and big names because the script and plot were terrible. If the movie showed up on the rental shelves too soon, then he concluded it didn't last in the box office very long because, of course, it was terrible. If there were too many copies available on the shelves, then that meant nobody wanted it because it was terrible. And—he was firm on this one—nothing, ever, with Woody Allen's name listed as an actor, director, producer, or endorser.

Add to this list of Robb's rules that I invariably, without fail, chose poorly. But a bad movie is still a movie, and I wanted to watch them. I had this idea that we would be a couple who watched a movie after bedtime, on the weekends, on date nights. That we would talk afterward about what it meant, I would compare it to the book without remotely expecting him to read it, and when the Oscars came around, we would have half an idea of what was going on. We were not that couple. There are certain things you come to terms with in marriage.

But I'm reinventing myself in this chapter of my life, and guess what? The new me? She watches movies. And you can't go wrong with *Annie*.

I popped popcorn, filled cups with orange juice, pulled the couch into the middle of the living room, loaded up on pillows and blankets, dimmed the lights, and tapped into Netflix. This was the evening I would introduce the boys to Annie, in all her curly charm. My brother and I watched this movie on a seemingly endless loop. (My mom thinks she may have watched it once in its entirety. This blesses me deeply to realize that she had other things to do while we were watching TV.) The lyrics and dialogue are hidden in my subconscious, and they emerged all throughout the evening. Thankfully, the boys don't yet believe this kind of commentary takes away from the movie experience. They were simply impressed that I seemed to know Annie's friends. We streamed Netflix through the Wii, and the movie sometimes got ahead of the downloading process. So we had to be patient while the screen paused to "retrieve." About the tenth time we were staring at a still screen, I was the one who became impatient. Surprisingly, the boys were really fine with the wait.

Tyler said, "Mommy, this is not that bad. You know what's bad? Touching hot lava. This isn't that bad."

True. Thank you for the perspective.

There's so much to love about Annie, not the least of which is the charisma of her short curls. I had just gotten a haircut, and the boys weren't receiving it well. I'm big on women's lib when it comes to hair. I think it's ultimately a woman's decision since the hair resides, after all, on her scalp.

When I have said this, some have asked me, "But, Tricia, don't you think marriage is a team effort? Don't you think it's a joint decision?"

I'd say I'm 55/45 on the percentages of authority over her hair, the extra points belonging to the girl. I mean, it's her hair. And to be fair, I kept mine long for a lot of years because the man in my life adored the curly locks, so I can't say I haven't been swayed by the opinion of another. But if a girl wants to cut her hair, I think she should do it.

I made a dramatic change by getting only a few inches cut off my hair. I loved it; my boys hated it. Tyler actually booed me while I sat in the stylist's chair.

"Tyler, let's have a talk about girls. Someday you'll have a girlfriend of your very own, and she needs to be allowed to wear her hair however she chooses. Maybe long, maybe short, maybe long and short—whatever she chooses. And even if you don't love it, you will love her, so it's a great idea to have something kind to say about how she looks. So let's try this again. What do you think of my hair, Tyler?"

He hesitated. "Boo."

Okay, then. Mental note to my future daughter-in-law: I'm working hard on this for you. Taking one for the team, if you will.

As Tucker climbed onto the couch next to me on movie night, I worked on my case by pointing to the curly-headed girl on the screen. I said, "Guys, look how cute Annie is. Her hair is short and curly like mine."

"Mommy, I'm not trying to be mean when I say this, but you just look so weird."

Awesome. Just watch the movie.

The thing about Annie is that she brings with her the word *orphan.* She gives us things to talk about. Questions to ask. And we are in the stage where the boys talk their way through movies to make sense of the plot and connect the dots.

"Mommy, Annie misses her mom and dad because they died. She wears that necklace because it reminds her of them."

"She lives in a big house for little girls because she doesn't have anyone else to take care of her."

"Why are mommies girls?" Tyler asked me, his eyes on the screen but his questions coming from somewhere else.

"Because God made us that way."

"Yes, but why? I want to know why you are a girl."

I wasn't sure how far we were going to take this: philosophy, anatomy. This question leads in many directions.

"When I was a baby inside Grandma, God decided that he wanted me to be a girl. And girls are the ones who grow up to be mommies."

Tucker piped in, "Yes, and when God made you into a girl, he had two little boys on his mind. He thought, 'I want to make two very good brothers, so I need to make their mommy now.'"

Just when I think he's not listening, he drops a nugget like that in my lap. *You are right, sweet Tuck. When God made me, he was thinking about you.*

They were captivated by Annie's story, her dog, Sandy, and of course the mysterious nature of Punjab. They woke me the next morning to say, "Mommy, let's talk about Annie." They found their due love for her, even if her hair is short. I think it probably doesn't hurt that her name is written in the sky with fireworks.

nineteen

It was the first wedding without Robb. The first wedding with my boys in company. The first wedding at which the bride was a single mom. I prepped the boys with promises of grandeur if they obeyed and stayed near me at all times and with threats against life as they know it if we needed to leave early for any reason related to their behavior. "Guys, we're getting out of the car, so wedding behavior starts *now*."

As we entered the church, a tuxedoed usher greeted us and offered me his arm. My little ducklings followed closely behind. We took our seats in a wooden pew, and I read the wedding program aloud. I explained words like *bridesmaids, groomsmen, flower girls, ring bearer, processional,* and the kiss. (They've got that last one figured out.)

The bride has seven brothers. One looks unbelievably like Robb, and of all the ironies, the bride told me that he was born on the same day, same year. His is the closest resemblance I have ever seen. I want to take his picture. I want to tell him why I can't stop looking at him.

The bride walks down the aisle to the tune of "Great Is Thy Faithfulness." Her daughter is one of our favorite babysitters; she cries as she watches her mom. I cry as I watch her. One of my life's pastors officiates the wedding. He officiated Robb's funeral. His voice is melodically familiar to me. I know the rise and fall. His family has carried mine. He speaks from a passage in Song of Solomon, a glimpse of love the way God intended. "May your love be as sure as death. Death is inevitable, something in this life that is sure to come our way. May your love be as lasting, as sure."

The boys whisper incessantly.

"Mommy, can we have a wedding someday?"

"Who will we sit with when you get married?"

"When you get married, I'll be the groom, Mommy."

"Mommy, are you crying because you are happy or sad?"

I'm really not sure. I think this is a both/and day.

The pastor talks about abiding love. Never missing a new word or phrase, Tyler calls out (loudly) from our row, "Biting love?!" Laughter sparkles around us. A friend whispers to her husband, "He's right. Sometimes it is biting love." Oh, Tyler. You bless me. The boys are unbelievably great. I keep them occupied with pens, paper, and chocolate-chip cookies.

"I have prayed for this day for years," the pastor tells us. He looks to the bride. "I have prayed for one person by name." He looks to the daughter of the bride. "I have prayed for another person by name." And he looks to the groom. "And I have prayed for one person in hope. And this day has finally come."

The bride and groom make vows to each other. And then they make vows to their daughter: a family commitment. It is beyond-words beautiful to me.

"I now present to you a new creation, never before seen on planet Earth: Mr. and Mrs. Andy Shannon." I cheer and I cry. Two thumbs up to the bride. *You did it, girlfriend. And now you have someone by your side for all the rest. Beyond-words beautiful.*

As we were driving home, with the wedding fresh in our minds, Tuck said, "It seems so long before a wedding."

"Well, yes, it can be a long time. There can be a lot to do to make a wedding happen."

(Plus, your dad and I dated for about eighty-eight days before we got engaged, so a longer engagement was wise for us . . . though I would never in my life want to do that again. Especially now that I know what I'm missing in all that waiting. Nope. Never again if I can help it.)

"So how does all that work, Mommy? What takes so long?"

"Well, first, a boy and a girl—or a man and a woman—become good friends, and they decide they might like to spend more time together. So then they go on a date, where they have lots of conversation and do something fun together. And if it goes well, then they go on another date. And another one after that."

"You should do that, Mommy. Those 'date' things."

Well, yes, thank you. And I do. You just don't know everything in the world.

"And then when they've had lots of dates and lots of time together, they might decide they want to spend more time together, maybe every day for the rest of their lives. And that's when the man goes shopping for a diamond ring, and he gives it to his girl when he asks her to marry him."

Tuck pulled his fedora down over his face.

"What's wrong, buddy?"

"This is getting embarrassing. Please stop."

"Really?"

"Stop looking at me while you're talking about this."

"Can I keep talking and stop looking at you?"

"No. Just stop."

Okay. But we're just getting to the good parts.

If you're interested in dating a widow, one who is a single mom with two children she'd lay down her life for, don't lead with this line:

"You know, statistically, 60 percent of the prison community was raised in a home without a father. I mean, I'm just saying."

Yeah, don't start with that.

Because what I heard in that sentence is "If you don't get married soon, and especially if you don't get married soon *to me,* then your little boys are in grave danger of a future with a criminal history and imprisonment."

Well, that sounds a little more like a threat than a pick-up line. And in general, I don't find threats to be very attractive. Just a heads-up.

I mean, he had a strong point: the numbers seem daunting. But I need to remember that my children are not statistics. I don't need to listen to my fears, and I must not lose hope because of scary reports.

I look fervently—sometimes almost desperately—for kids of any age who have been raised by single moms. I want to see with my own eyes children who are confident, successful, and functioning without a dad in their lives. I want to see adults who are happily married, gainfully employed, and have not stolen cars, used drugs, or murdered people. I want someone to promise me that my boys will be okay, that we will be okay. I cling to any encouraging truth I can find, and when I found this quote from one of my favorite authors and psychologists, I scribbled it on a note and posted it on my bathroom mirror.

In his book *What a Difference a Mom Makes,* Kevin Leman wrote, "Although it might be natural to think that the man in your son's life . . . would have the most influence on him since they're both males, the opposite is true. *You* influence your son directly and have a much greater impact on the man he will become. . . . If you're a single parent and you're trying to be mom *and* dad, there's good news: you don't have to be both. . . . Just be his *mom,* and you can heap blessings on him for a lifetime."

I love the chronological Bible. It's more like reading a novel, like hearing things as they happened, in the order they happened, and hearing what everyone had to say about them no matter when they lived or died or prophesied. Seriously. Revolutionary to my biblical understanding.

Today I'm reading about the Sadducees (a.k.a. self-righteous punks who wanted to catch Jesus in a mistake and thereby strip him of all credibility) when they came to Jesus with the question about the widow. I love this 'cause I can just picture it.

They came to Jesus and said, "Teacher, Moses wrote for us that if a man's brother dies and leaves a wife but no children, the man must marry the widow and have children for his brother."

Let's take a moment and be thankful this rule is no longer in play. No need to go disrupting Robb's brother's family with a

second wife who wants to have more kids who would simultaneously become nieces and nephews and brothers and sisters and
daughters and sons. Have a crack at that family tree.

"Now there were seven brothers. The first one married the
woman and died childless. The second and then the third married
her . . ." Good grief! The poor woman of the story, widowed over
and over. And over. And the Sadducees don't stop there. Oh no.
Three dead husbands wouldn't be enough to illustrate the compli-
cation of the issue.

"And the same thing happened to all of the husbands, right
down to the seventh brother. Finally the woman died too."

I bet she sure did.

"At the resurrection, when all of these men are alive in heaven,
whose wife will she be of the seven, since all of them were married
to her?"

Jesus's first answer, paraphrased, is, "You're all wrong. You
don't know the Bible, and you don't know the power of God."

And that right there, I would think, is reason enough to stop
asking him the complicated math questions. Because he's going to
keep calling you out with his wise answers, you ding-dongs.

Then Jesus gives them his answer: "In heaven, people will
neither marry nor be given in marriage."

His next sentence says, "They will be like angels," and since I
don't really understand what that means, I'm going to focus on
the first part: no marriage in heaven.

This never made sense to me in my married years. I was so
puzzled. Why would God give this man to me—only me—on
earth if in heaven he'll belong to anyone and everyone? Why don't

the married years count, like an investment you get to cash in when you get to heaven?

But I get it now, at least with a little more clarity.

I think the ultimate goal of marriage is pure intimacy. It's knowing each other from across the room, knowing the history and the preferences, remembering what he's good at and what her gifts are. It's the purity of loving each other in an untainted place, where nobody can change your mind about how much you love this person. And I think we get a taste of heaven in an earthly relationship where we know each other inside and out, we continue to learn about each other, and we are perpetually interested in learning more.

In heaven maybe this kind of intimacy will be true in every relationship. At first that baffles me, making me feel like all my relationships will run together if they are defined the same way.

But then I think about how I have no two friendships that are the same, no two friends who bring the same kinds of joy and presence to my life, no person who is replaceable with someone else. And I see how all these unique shades and hues bring color to my life.

So if that's the case in heaven, if I will know how to love everyone with a holy, sacred intimacy, and if they in turn will love me to the same degree, and we all get to hang out with Jesus and have great meals and amazing parties, then sign me up.

twenty

W hy would anyone want to step into this? We are a horrible mess."

"Oh, Trish, you are not a horrible mess." My friend Laurelyn's voice was gentle and compassionate. "I think you've got a lot going on, but you are not a horrible mess."

Bless her sweet heart for believing this is true. Because I mostly feel like we are a mess.

To me, it feels like chaos abounds. To me, it feels like I'd escape if I could. To me, it feels like no one in his right mind would want to step into this with us. Why would someone want to step out of a peaceful stride and into the lane with scooters and wagons and Band-Aids? I am afraid that we are unlovable. I am afraid that we cannot be mended. Mostly, I am just afraid.

It is one of my greatest fears and deepest prayers: *Please, God, let there be someone who can want to step into life with us, love my children with a supernatural love, choose the challenges of parenting, and somehow also love me with abandon. Let there be someone whose stride I can join, someone who is pointed in the same direction, that we may join hands and do this together.*

My mom says, "Tricia, this is truly not that big a miracle. Greater things have happened." She says this with a gentle smile, the heart of a mother, the perspective of unconditional love. I suspect she cannot think any other way. Still, this feels like a feat of all feats, an outlandish dream. As I was lying in my bed last night, scriptures came rushing to my mind, dancing around in my thoughts, like a child begging to be noticed.

"With God, all things are possible." And the converse, "Nothing is impossible with God." Oddly, I kind of lean toward the one with the double negative. Shortly after those, these words were written across my mind: "Test me. Try me and see if I will fill your warehouses with blessing."

It is not impossible. It is not impossible that I will be loved. It is not impossible for God to place within a man a supernatural, paternal love for my children. It is not impossible that someone can love our mess. It is not impossible.

And then I am prompted to think, *What else* was not *impossible?* It was not impossible that I would become an author. It was not impossible for my agent to find me. It was not impossible for there to be a bidding war over who would buy my words. It was not impossible that you would choose, this minute, to read the meanderings of my thoughts.

It was not impossible that my home sold in fifteen days, that I found a new home immediately and purchased it just under the wire, that this home is ours and made for us, no matter who lived here before. It was not impossible that I have lived, continue to live.

And so I have begun a list. Two lists. (I'm tempted to pull out my teaching supplies and make an interactive bulletin board in my home.)

It was not impossible for God to . . .

and

It is not impossible for God to . . .

I am writing each "impossible" on a three-by-five card, placing it under the category where it belongs, and believing that someday each of these cards will belong under the heading "Was Not Impossible." Greater miracles have happened.

I went to bed at 6:45 last night. My brain had stopped thinking, my heart was overwhelmed, and I could not seem to think through the steps of homework and bedtime, let alone navigate them. (Insert my mom, ever the hero. She came to think and navigate on my behalf.) I lay in my bed, not even asleep, but just needing to be still. A preemptive approach to fighting anxiety. It was threatening its arrival, so I was barring the windows and locking the doors. I could hear my mom. "Boys, let's read these two books, and then you need to finish your homework and put on jammies."

"But will there be bedtime TV tonight?"

"Not tonight."

"But Mommy said there will be."

"Mommy doesn't feel well tonight, so she's in bed. We're going to read two books, finish homework, and put on jammies." Tyler argued her to the moon and back, and she pulled out the maternal voice she needs for such situations, the one I learned to heed thirty years ago. He obeyed.

Tucker was compliant but terrified. Mommy's sick? Mommy's in bed? He snuck up to my room. His sweet face . . . his firm jaw, his quivering chin, his teary eyes. "Mommy? You're sick?"

"Buddy, I'm okay. I'm just going to bed early tonight. I need to take a break."

"Mommy, I'm just so afraid. Sometimes my mind thinks you're going to be dead." I sat up to show him that I could and to make direct eye contact with him.

"Lovey, I'm not dying. I promise you."

"You can't say that. Because everyone will die. You're going to get old and die."

"That's true. But I'm here. And I won't leave you for as long as you need me."

"As long as I'm a kid, I need you, Mommy."

I know, lovey. I'm here. I'm here. I promise. I'm here.

He read the two books, finished his homework, got into his jammies, and tried to be brave.

My mom came to my room to check on me and deliver the update. "Tyler's looking for things to do, and Tucker's very worried."

"Should I go in there?"

"Well, I do think it would save us all some time and heartache. But be sure to look healthy." Easy to do. I'm healthy. Just weary to my core. I went into the boys' room, and at the mere sight of me, Tucker burst into wailing tears. He just couldn't stop crying. He grasped at me, my hands, my neck. Oh, the terror in his heart.

On the bottom bunk Tyler was situating his stuffed animals, piling them on top of and around him, covering them with blankets and blankets and blankets. His own coping mechanism.

"Hey, guys, everybody up. Come to my room."

"For just a little while, Mommy?"

"No, for the night. Come on down."

Tyler brought his entire community of plush toys and soft

blankets, and he made a nest on the floor next to my bed. Tucker climbed right into the spot that was Robb's, and he asked if he could please have his hand on my arm all night. "I just need to know you're there." I know, sugar.

My mom tucked us all in and slipped out, setting the security alarm on her way, and my boys and I had another sleepover in my room last night. It definitely defeated the purpose of my early bedtime, but there is no greater cause than to help my sons feel safe. For this, I will take interruptions and wandering hands and feet and snoring and sleep talking and the sweet breathing rhythm of boys asleep.

Tuck woke in the middle of the night, crying and crying. This doesn't happen to us as often anymore.

"What's wrong, buddy?" I rubbed his back.

"I don't know. I just don't know why I'm crying." And then, "Mommy, why don't you cry for my daddy anymore?"

Oh, sweet boy. I think I know why you're crying. And I think I might not have words to explain it either. "I still do sometimes, Tuck. I cry when I'm sad, but I'm not always sad. It's okay if you want to cry, and it's okay if you don't. You can feel however you feel, buddy."

Just feel how you feel, my love. It's all I've learned how to do.

He fell back to sleep, and daylight finally found us.

Good morning, boys. Look. I'm still here.

twenty-one

Look at that alien, Mommy. He only has one eye."

"True. One big one."

"I think God only has one eye, Mommy. Do you think he has one or two?"

"Well, we were made to look like him, and we have two, so I think he has two."

"Can he see us?"

"Always."

"Can Daddy see us?"

"I'm not sure, Tyler. Maybe sometimes."

"Can he hear us?"

"Well, I'm not sure, but I talk to him sometimes, and you can talk to him if you want to."

His eyes dart around the room, silently exploring the parameters of the life we know.

Almost inaudibly he whispers, "Hey, Daddy? Could you come back, please?"

When I hear his voice again, he says, "Camels store water in their humps."

Then he begins to pepper me with a barrage of facts. "Meat-eating dinosaurs eat other dinosaurs and even their blood. Also, Pluto is a dog at Disney World, and it's also a planet. And stars are red and yellow and blue even though they look white in the sky.

And also, Mommy, you never heared any of these things before."
(That's not a typo; it's Tyler vernacular. Not *heard*. "Heared.")

For a moment I think to debate with him, to tell him that I
too learned these things when I was his age (or older, if I'm honest). *Believe it or not, sweet child, you have a smart mommy.*

But wisdom says let him tell you. Just let him tell you his
discovery. And I do. "Tell me more, Tyler."

"Strawberries grow in springtime, Mommy. And ants don't
have eyes, but they have antennae." His facts and tidbits are endless. He is my fact finder, storing tiny snippets in his mind. His
brother is more of an explorer, digging in and figuring out how
something works and perhaps never saying it out loud. Tyler wants
to know how it sounds; Tucker wants to see it in action.

His list of facts leads me to recall the pages of my journal this
morning. I've been thinking on my new discoveries: *God is patient with me. We are more than conquerors. Healing is in your
hands. Nothing is gained through hurry. Nothing, nothing. God is
the anchor for my soul; I will not float away. I am betrothed. His
promises are true, he means what he says, and he is in this moment
with me. Here. Now. Slow down. Engage. Don't wish this season
away. There is much fruit here. Taste and see.* And I write it all
down, my version of Tyler's dinner conversation. I talk about
what I'm learning, just as Tyler does. He tosses words around,
says them every way he knows. I doodle in the margins; I play
with the words; I let my pen dance around the page.

He and I are both learning. I listen to Tyler, careful not to
interrupt, ready to hear what has crossed his mind today. His
learning is new to him, even if it isn't new information to me.

And suddenly I realize: perhaps God delights in my discoveries too. He knows he is patient, all knowing, present, hearing, constant, and mine. And as I discover these things—sometimes for the first time, sometimes anew once more—he lets me say it. He lets me tell him. Even though it's not new to him.

God's not saying, "Right. I know. Who do you think wrote the book you found it in? Nice try, kiddo. Tell me something I don't know." He listens and delights as I learn who he is.

Tonight at the dinner table I'll say, "Hey, somebody tell me what you learned today. Go."

And tomorrow, over my cup of coffee, God will whisper the same thing to me. *What'd you learn today, daughter of mine?*

And then Tyler wrapped it up. "Well, I think I'll just go outside and ride my bike for a while." He says this so casually, as if it were the most normal thing in the world. As if I hadn't needed to pay him to pedal ten times the last time we gave this a try.

He was dressed in long sleeves and long pants, kneepads and elbow pads—ones that were mine from my rollerblading days—and a helmet that has never been his or I haven't been paying attention to how small his head is.

If I'm honest, I wasn't really in the mood for bike riding. Despite the clothing Tyler chose, it was ninety-three degrees, and I had had just about enough of being hot. But when your strong-willed child chooses a battle, or in this case a victory, you rarely get a voice in choosing the perfect timing. So out we went.

I encouraged him, "Buddy, you really did a lot of the hard

work last time. The hardest part is learning to balance, and your body knows how to do that now. There's this saying, 'It's like riding a bike,' and that means it's something you never forget how to do. Once your body learns the balance of riding a bike, then you're golden. I think you're about to surprise yourself with how easy this is going to be."

He looked at me with his eyelids half-mast, as if encouragement was the very last thing he needed right now. His eyes said, *Just hold on to the bike seat, please.* And wouldn't you know it, he took off. I sort of thought that might happen. Because isn't that how parenting goes almost nine times out of ten? You push and pull, you aim and prod, and you try to make them think it was their idea all along, and then one day they just . . . do it. And the waiting feels like nothing at all.

I think God feels the same way about me.

I used to think I wanted to be with a man who had it figured out. Then I found that often means his life is black and white with little room for gray.

I used to think I wanted as many kids and pregnancies as my body could withstand. Then I learned that *can* and *should* are not synonymous.

I used to think I'd teach elementary school forever. Then I got a taste of teaching adults and discovered my favorite thing in the world.

I used to think that shared finances meant "weekly allowance." Then I learned it doesn't have to.

I used to think I was not much of a housewife. Then I learned that a housewife and a homemaker are not the same thing.

I used to think I didn't know how to decorate. Then I made my home beautiful.

I used to think a man and woman should share everything. Then I learned how much more I have to offer when some things are only mine.

I used to think marriage was the only route for me. Then I began to wonder if I'll ever want to do it again.

I used to think I would feel most secure with someone who had the answers. Then I realized how beautiful are the words "You know what, honey? I don't know."

I used to think I didn't love movies. Then I started watching the ones I wanted to see.

I used to think that changing myself for someone else was like stretching a rubber band. Then I learned it's more like molding clay.

I used to think my intelligence and autonomy were a currency I could afford to spend. Then I learned that's not true. At all.

I used to think I was half. Then I learned I've been whole all along.

Part Six

let's start right here

twenty-two

"Mommy, where are Daddy's bones?" Tuck asks me.

We're in the car, where most of our pivotal conversations happen. He asks me this question with an authoritative tone that dares me to keep this secret, and just like all the other moments when I knew it was time to talk about the topic at hand, I know it's time to talk about this.

But it's something of a complicated question to answer since Robb chose to be cremated. I don't know how to say those words, or I don't want to.

"Well, buddy, your dad knew that he would leave his entire body behind when he died."

Sometimes I find that I call him "your dad" now instead of "Daddy" since Tucker stands taller than my chin, and it seems like a transition we should make even though Robb's not here.

"He knew his body would be just an empty shell with no part of him in it at all, and he decided that he wanted his bones to be turned into rocks and scattered in the mountains."

Both boys are listening, and they seem to be thankful for honesty and respect. Which I intend to always give them. Always.

"So after he died, they gave me a box filled with rocks and sand, stones and ashes. I took the rocks to a mountain lake that your dad loved, and I sprinkled them into the sand by the water."

"And that's where his bones are?"

"That's where his bones are."

"Mommy, can we go there? Can we go to that lake? And can we touch the sand? Please?"

Yes, my loves. We can.

"I wish I had died when Daddy died."

"Why?"

"Because don't you know I haven't seen him since I was five? Don't you know that's such a long time?"

"It is a long, long time. You are terribly right."

Tucker has come to a new awareness of the dad-void in his life. He talks about it much, cries about it easily, and has a bitter-sweet relationship with pictures and memories. He says, "I want to look at that, but . . . I just can't." He shrugs tears back even though he doesn't have to.

"I just wish I had died."

"I can understand that. I've wished that sometimes too. But the thing is, once you go to heaven, you can't come back. That's why Daddy isn't here."

"I know."

I know you know. I'm not trying to patronize you. You know all too well, my love.

"So if you died too, I'd be here without you. And then I'd look around and think, 'Well, now what am I supposed to do?'"

That makes him smile. My tall boy.

What I love most is that he can tell me things like this, tell me that death doesn't scare him and sometimes sounds okay. It's not the same as wanting to end his life; it's the longing to go home.

Because to us, it's very real. And probably a lot like stepping into a room you've never seen before.

"But just think. Someday you'll get to go, and Daddy will be ready for you. And you'll get to introduce him to your wife and your children, and he will love to see everything you did while you were here. He doesn't mind waiting for you. So go ahead and stick around. With me. Capeesh?"

"Capeesh."

"Mommy, can I take my blanket with me to heaven?" Tyler's face is snuggled into his blue blanket, satin and plush, the love of his life for nearly eight years now.

"Well, when you get to heaven, God will give you a new one if that's what you need."

He ponders this. He studies his blanket, threadbare and stained.

"Will the new one have stains? Because I have these two stains from juice and hot chocolate."

I think of the many things I'm told will be spotless, without blemish.

"It will be perfect. No stains."

He thinks more on this. Traces the stains with his long fingers.

"Mommy, I don't want a new one. I want this one. Can't I just take this one?"

I have to be honest: we were nearing bedtime, and I was painfully aware that if I told this child God would not allow him to bring his blanket into heaven, neither of us would get any sleep that night. Also, I would give my son a portrait of a jealous God who is unforgiving and without grace for the items of comfort in our life.

So I reminded myself of all the things I don't know. And maybe all those who say "You can't take it with you" . . . maybe they don't know either. Maybe Tyler will look down at his new hands, and he'll see his beloved blanket, stained and loved. I don't know. Maybe.

Maybe he'll be ninety-five years old by then, and he'll search his memory for why this blanket mattered to him in the first place. I don't know. Maybe.

If I were a legalist, I would say, "Absolutely no way that filthy blanket is making it to heaven, and you must not sleep with your blanket for forty nights because obviously it has become an idol in your life."

Good thing I'm not a legalist, then. That's a lot of sleepless nights for everyone involved.

The question behind the question is actually "Mommy, will I feel safe in heaven?"

"Sure, buddy. You can take it."

"I can? I can take this blanket to heaven?" He holds it up to me just to clarify. This blanket. This one right here.

"Sure."

"So, Mommy,"—again, just to clarify—"when Jesus comes down on a cloud of angels, I can run and get my blanket?"

"Sure, buddy."

God knows his heart—and mine. And I think when it comes

time to prove who was right or wrong, we'll have greater things on our minds.

"I don't want to drink my milk. I don't want to grow. I don't want to get too heavy. I don't want to get bigger."

At first glance these are alarming sentences from a child. Eating disorder? Body image issues, less common in boys but still possible? *God, help me . . . does he not want to live anymore?* I probed gently into these topics, maintaining an expression of zero concern. I didn't want him to put his words away if he thought the sight of them would scare me.

"Tell me more about that, buddy."

"I don't want to grow because I don't want to be too big when I get to heaven. If I'm too big, then I can't play horsey with Daddy. I wish I could just die now, while I'm still small, while he can still lift me."

Oh, Tyler. My heart breaks with the things that worry you.

"Buddy, I have good news: in heaven every daddy can hold his son. It doesn't matter how big you are or how old he is. None of that matters there. You can wrestle and play, climb all over him, and he'll know just who you are and how you love to play."

"So I can drink my milk?"

"You can drink your milk."

twenty-three

I have often likened this grief journey to having a newborn. When I think back on those first six months of being a widow, there are some striking similarities to those first months of being a mom. Schedules, routines, and familiarity were upturned; there was little to do but sleep; I spent much time remembering the day it all changed. I could never forget the day Robb died, but I began to think about it less. There were more milestones waiting as I learned to walk and laugh again.

When Tucker was born, my heart was overwhelmed with a consuming love for this little person, this complete little boy who had grown inside me, just beneath my heart. I studied him as a newborn, the cowlick that matches mine (straight up from the inside of his right eyebrow), the dimpled hands, the sounds of his cries that carried subtle meanings, a language all our own. I fell in love. I began to wrap my mind around this enchantment, this undeniable bond that carried me through even our stir-crazy days. My heart was full.

And when I became pregnant with Tyler, I feared that my heart couldn't possibly contain any more joy, any more love. How could I love another one as much?

And then I met Tyler. And on the very day he was born, I realized how foolish my fears had been. Of course I could love this one—just as much. I studied him as a newborn, also with the cowlick that matches mine, the long and slender feet, the pointed chin, the red hair. And my heart was full . . . fuller than before.

I am learning that the heart has no maximum capacity for joy. There is always room for more. It's not made up of percentages, portions to divide, or pieces to share accordingly. Joy is one big mess of affections, each overlapping into another and yet each still with strands all its own. Parents with many, many children say the same. Your home may reach its capacity, but your heart never will. There's always room for one more.

But I assert that pain is quite the opposite. I believe that the heart has a limitation for pain and that the body can handle only so much. I have read stories of people struck with hypothermia; they feel cold, painfully cold, freezing cold, and then they don't feel anymore. The limbs that are frozen stop hurting. They have been wounded too deeply to feel it any longer. And in the most severe cases, those who nearly die in a blizzard say that a warmth comes over them, a cozy calling to sleep. Burns to the skin are rated by degree: first, second, and third. Third-degree burns are so severe that they destroy the nerve endings; the injured one stops feeling the pain.

I think my heart has a capacity for pain, a limit to the hurt it will hold. Emptiness has its boundary; it is possible to feel so poured out that there seems nothing left to lose.

In those darkest months I think I reached my capacity. I think of other things that could go wrong in my life, other dreams that may someday be shattered by death. While a different loss would present a different angle, a different lens, I'm not sure it could hurt more. I'm not sure I can hurt more. The brain and body must cope somehow. I may someday hurt differently. But I'm not sure I could hurt more.

And there is a third facet to my contention: as the wound begins to heal, as joy begins to return, as I begin to feel again and anew, my heart begins to feel the pain that comes with joy. In the face of joy, in the warmth of healing, I realize just how deep this wound has gone. And it hurts. As a person begins to thaw from hypothermia, as feeling returns, it brings excruciating pain. It is part of the journey.

I am learning my heart's capacity: the spill of joy, the outpouring of emptiness, the pain of both. I am learning.

I was reading to the boys from *The Jesus Storybook Bible,* which happens to be my very favorite version of Bible stories. These are far and above the best retellings of the stories that shaped the foundation of what I believe. It's written for children, but good writing is good writing, and I find myself falling in love with the stories all over again—or some for the first time—as I read them aloud to my children.

It was bedtime, and together we were reading the story of Abraham and Isaac. I was well into reading it aloud before I realized that maybe this particular story is better processed during the day instead of at bedtime with its images of a father climbing a hill with his young son, tying him down on an altar, and raising a knife to offer him as a sacrifice. My boys' eyes grew wider as we got closer and closer to the end of the story, and they breathed an audible exhale when they heard God relent at the last minute and spare Isaac's life.

At best this is one of the more troubling stories of the Old Testament. Tucker said, "I am so confused right now. Why would God do that? Why would God ask Abraham to kill his son?"

"Well, buddy, I don't understand this story completely, but I think it's because God had a very, very important job for Abraham to do. And he needed to know that Abraham would trust him and obey him, no matter what, even if it didn't make sense to him. And when he saw that Abraham would obey, then he didn't make Abraham actually kill his son."

"So God rescued Isaac. And he didn't make Abraham give him up."

I watched him trying to connect the dots. "That's right."

"Mommy, do you think you are like Abraham?"

Tyler interrupted. "Tucker, she doesn't want to kill us."

"I *know* that. It's not what I mean." He glanced to the ceiling in exasperation over the people in his life he must deal with. "But, Mommy, do you think God has an important job for you to do? And that's why he asked you to give up my dad?"

I had no words. Even now as I remember him telling me his insight, I have no words.

In my silence he continued. "Mommy, do you know God has picked you to write these books? He made you a writer to tell these stories. And so maybe God had to know you would trust him no matter what."

Good grief. Who is this child teaching me theology in my bedroom?

"But here's what I don't understand, Mom. If God rescued Isaac once he saw that Abraham would obey, why didn't he rescue my dad?"

Tucker was all questions, and Tyler was all ears right alongside his brother.

"I don't know, honey. I've asked God that question almost every day. Sometimes I get pretty angry with God over the whole thing."

He looked at me with pleading eyes, and his voice was gentle. "Mommy, no. Please don't be mad at God. I don't want you to go to hell."

"Oh, Tuck! That's not how it works, buddy. I won't go to hell for asking questions." I stroked his face and saw once again how he's becoming less little boy and more young man.

"Honey, God lets us feel how we feel, and he lets us ask him questions. In fact, there's a place in the Bible where David reminds us to tell God every one of our concerns. That means we can tell him anything we are feeling. And sometimes I miss your dad so much, and it makes me so sad that you don't have him, and I wish God would have made a different decision on that day. So I tell him."

It is impossibly heartbreaking to be so vulnerable in front of my children, to watch their faces reflect the conclusion that some of their greatest questions have no answers, to let them see that I just don't know.

"Come here, guys. Let me tell you something." They climbed into bed with me. I wrapped my arms around them, and I told them what I think is true.

"You guys, your dad could have died twenty years earlier. When he was in his sledding accident and his spleen ruptured, he could have died right then. But I think God thought, 'If Robb Williford comes to heaven on this day, then Tricia Lott won't get to marry him. And if Robb and Tricia don't get married, then Tucker and Tyler will never be born. I need those boys to be born because I need the world to have what they can bring.'"

My children were crying. I held them close, and I forged ahead.

"I think God wants to show people your friendship with each other. And he needs your hearts and your tenderness and your compassion. He needs you to play sports and tell stories. He needs you to make friends and love people. He wanted you here, so he let Robb Williford live long enough to become your dad."

"Really, Mommy?"

"Really. And I think he thought, 'I'll have Robb stay for another twenty years. It won't feel very long for Tricia, and it sure won't be very long for Tucker and Tyler, but it will be long enough for what I want to do.'"

"Are we here so Daddy could die?"

"No, baby. I think he lived so you could be born."

"It makes me so sad, Mommy."

"I know, sugar. Me too."

I wrapped a blanket around the mound of us, and we cried. And I told God how we felt, right then and there so my boys could listen.

God, help me.

twenty-four

I'm so glad Daddy taught us about beans before he died."

"Beans?" *Of all things?*

"Yes, you know. How they make you toot."

This is what they remember. And I know Robb would be so proud that this information stuck.

"What else did he teach you? Let's see if we can name five things."

"He taught us how to pee in a toilet."

"Very true. And I am forever thankful."

"He taught us how to drink from a bottle of water without spilling it everywhere. Like you don't put your mouth over the whole top of the bottle."

"He taught us to respect girls. And to be gentle with them."

He taught you the beauty of boy humor;

he demonstrated the benefits of standing to pee—a concept I assuredly cannot appreciate;

he taught you how to drink like a man;

and he showed you how he loved me.

Not a bad legacy.

Seven years ago when I started the blog, I wrote for myself. I wrote for the precious hour during naptime when I could think for a few minutes on my own. I wrote to think out loud, and I wrote to remember. I wrote to remember that I could think.

Why did I write about my children? Because they were my days and nights, my waking and sleeping, my happiness and my exhaustion.

I wrote about them because I was learning, from them and about them, and thereby so much about myself, and I think anything I learn is worth writing down, even if I'm the only one who reads it. Sometimes, especially if I am the only one who reads it.

Recently I've been under scrutiny for writing about my kids.

"You're exploiting them. You're disrespectful."

"We grieve for the day they learn what you have said."

"You don't understand who they will be when they are teenagers, how they will likely never forgive you."

One of my longstanding hopes is that women will share the mutual respect that we're all doing our best, that there's no room for judgment, and that knowing more about one another offers greater support for each of us.

I don't think I actually need to explain this to anyone but my children, but I'll say it anyway. We have a system of rules in our home, and a series of them apply to the things we say or do not say outside our home. There are things we don't say to neighbors or classmates or even grandparents. There are things I don't write on Facebook or on the blogosphere or in a book manuscript. And there is a question we ask each other mutually and often: "Can I talk about this? Or should I keep this private and in our family?" And if any one of us says no, or even hesitates to say yes, then we have our collective answer.

I continue to write about them and us and life and happiness and exhaustion. The first two years of life without Robb would be gone, completely and forever, from my memory if I had not written down the story. I can't remember those days. The life of those days exists only in the words I wrote when I was writing to breathe. Everything else has fallen into the abyss of memories the mind tries to erase.

Why do I write about my children? So that someday I can tell my children that I did the best I could. I write about them as the most tangible way to learn what I am made of, to learn who this fierce woman is who has been struck down but not destroyed, who lives only because she loves.

Someday they will say, "Mom, what was it like after Dad died? What was it like when we were small? Was it hard for you? What did depression look like and feel like? How did we process it all? What did we say? How did you help us? How did you even know what to do?"

And I will say, "Here, baby. I wrote it down for you."

I love a cold house. Like, ridiculously so. My bedroom at night is downright cold. A certain Robb Williford is to blame for this. I had no choice but to adapt my body temperature to his arctic preferences.

But the furnace stopped working yesterday, a Sunday, and the temp in the house was dropping dangerously close to my age. I'm a tough girl, but this I can't handle. So we loaded up and went to my parents' house, which meant three things: (1) Tuck could watch the Broncos with his favorite comrade, Grandma; (2) favorite cereals for everyone; (3) waking up to my dad's coffee.

It also meant that Tuck and I would be bunkmates. I came to bed after he had fallen asleep, so I nudged him to move over and make room for me. He looked at me with narrow, sleepy eyes and pillow creases across his cheek. "Um, no, Mommy. I'm going to sleep on this side. Sorry about that."

I forgive you. And I'll sleep on the far side.

"Mommy, can I have that fuzzy blanket you brought up?"

"No, because you get to sleep on that side."

He rolled over to face me, now fully awake. He looked at the book in my hands, *Lots of Candles, Plenty of Cake* by Anna Quindlen. (Love. Her.)

"Mommy, what does that say across the top? Number One . . . New . . . York . . . Tim's . . . Boat Stealer."

"Close. Actually it says 'Number 1 *New York Times* Bestseller.' The *New York Times* is a newspaper, and they keep track of the books people love most. That means this is a book that America loves."

He traced the letters. I said, "That's one of my dreams, Tuck. I would love for one of my books to say that on the cover."

He held the book out to me. "Well, look! You already have a book that says that!"

"No, I mean a book that I write. I hope someday one of the books I have written will be a *New York Times* bestseller."

"Ohhhhh . . ." A look of recognition. Aha. So it's not just about collecting NYTBS, although there is great merit in that.

He opened my book, naturally filled with doodles and notes,

circles and scalloped underlines. He said, almost out of the side of his mouth as if he were speaking a secret we keep together, "Mommy, I told my teacher about this. I told her that you write in books."

"Oh, did you?"

"Yes. I told her I think you underline the very best sentences and probably also any words you don't know." The second-grade version of "interacting with the text."

I smiled. "Yep. That's pretty much how it goes, buddy. Do you ever write in books?"

My rule follower looked at me wide eyed. "No. I definitely do not."

I situated my pillow under my head as he found my bookmark, a three-by-five card with one of my favorite quotes scripted in my handwriting. He asked me to read it to him.

"It says, 'Life is a collection of a million, billion moments, tiny little moments and choices, like a handful of luminous, glowing pearls. It takes so much time, and so much work, and those beads and moments are so small, and so much less fabulous and dramatic than the movies.' It's written by Shauna Niequist, one of my favorite authors."

He rolled onto his back and said, "A million moments."

I think this was one of them.

twenty-five

Guys, let me tell you what I'm thinking about today."

Tyler is coloring the space between the tiles on the table at Chili's, and Tucker is looking like something straight out of the 1930s in his Easter hat. He looks like a newsy.

We have just finished an evening at church; we opted to go on Saturday so our parking spot would be free tomorrow for someone who might come for the first time. This has led to many conversations of clarity, since we went to church on Good Friday and again on Holy Saturday, even though Easter is on Sunday.

Just put on your hats and join me, newsies.

"I have been thinking about Easter. Please tell me why we celebrate it." Please tell me an accurate answer.

Earlier this week they were caught up in Easter eggs and bunnies, and I swallowed a gulp of maternal shame since their priorities were clearly off target. So we've been rehearsing a bit each day. Please learn these answers, even if they're only words to you right now.

They recite the answers, thankfully in their own words. "Easter is the day that Jesus rose from the dead after he died on the cross. Jesus is the only one who rose from the dead three days later, just like he said he would, so this is the way we can know Jesus is the real thing."

"You got it."

There's a fine line between pride and responsibility. It's my responsibility to teach them well; I am proud of them when they know the answers.

"Here's what I was thinking about that, guys. If Jesus hadn't risen from the dead, then there would be no way for us to get to heaven. That's where Daddy is. And that's where we will go when this life is over because we believe Jesus is the real thing. Everybody gets to go if they believe him. So we will get to see Daddy again."

"Because Daddy is going to come alive again?"

"No, sugar. He's gone for good. Jesus is the only one who came back. But since Jesus came back, he showed us there's more after this. When people die, they don't just stop. This isn't all there is."

"Mommy, if there wasn't heaven, people would have to sleep for a long, long time." True. And I'll choose right now not to go into any theories on existentialism or purgatory. Which is wise also because I don't know very much about either one. "And that would just be so boring. Lying around waiting to be buried."

We all agree: dying just for the sake of death would be boring and pointless. As a collective three, we're not up for that.

"Guys, because of Easter, we get to see Daddy again. Because this isn't all there is."

"I want to go now, Mommy."

"I know, lovey. But we'll live as many days as God gives us, just like Daddy did. And then, when we're done, it will only get better."

This is the most tangible understanding of the Resurrection that I've ever claimed.

We celebrate with our family, with our community, with believers all over the world, and with Daddy and his many friends in heaven.

We celebrate because this isn't all there is.

twenty-six

The boys point to a condominium complex as we drive past.

"Mommy, that's where Miss P. lives. But don't try to get in there, because you have to have a card. Like, see that thing by the gate at the entrance? It's a scanner, and you drive up and scan your card, and that's the only way you can get in."

"That's called a gated community. Your dad and I used to live in a place like that."

A couple of times, actually. The second address was so secure that I had a hard time getting home sometimes, but that was better than our first apartment, where the "gate" was so scant that it kept out only the people who didn't want to come in anyway.

"Did we live there with you?"

"No, it was before you were born."

"Oh, so we were inside you."

"No, I wasn't pregnant with you yet. You weren't here at all yet."

"So we were still in heaven? It's weird that we were ever in heaven, because I don't remember it at all."

"Well, I'm pretty sure you only started to exist when you were inside me. I don't think you lived anywhere before that."

"Okay, but God made us."

"He sure did. And he knew you were coming. And he knew your name and when you would arrive. And he has a special job for you to do while you're here. Did you know that?"

"What kind of special job?"

"Well, that's yours to figure out with God. But everybody is here with a very important job to do. God created you to do it, and it's only yours to do."

"What's yours?"

"Well, first of all, I'm your mom. It's my job to be your mom every day for all of your life, in all the ways you need me to. But I'm also a friend, and I'm a sister and a daughter, and I'm an author. I get to tell stories and write books for people to read, and my story becomes part of theirs."

"So that's your ending?"

That's kind of a harsh way to put it. "I hope it's not my ending. I hope I'm not finished anytime soon."

"But it's why you were made?"

"Yes. I think those are some of the reasons I was made."

"Well, I am made for sports," says the tall one, who is actually twice the weight of the smaller one. "I'm going to play football and teach kids to love that game. Tyler is made for . . . other things."

"Yeah, like science. And I'm going to invent medicines for people who try a cigarette and then they don't want it anymore. I think it will cost ten dollars. Or maybe fifty. Or it might be free."

Most days he vacillates between inventing drugs to cure addictions and imagineering Disney experiences.

And then we arrive at the park, and they run off to play, one to throw a ball high and long, and the other to experiment with combinations of sand and water to create the best consistency for a castle.

"Train up a child in the way he should go," the Bible says. So often I think we've misinterpreted this verse, perhaps focusing on the wrong word. I had always emphasized the word *way*—train up a child in the *way* he should go, and when he is old, he will not depart from it. There is only one Way, Truth, and Life; on this we can agree. But there are so many, many, many ways to teach a child to follow this narrow path.

I've learned a different way to read that verse: train up a child in the way *he* should go, and when he is old, he will not depart from it. Hear the difference? Your child is uniquely designed to think and behave on her own, to respond in her own way to the voice and influence of the Holy Spirit in her life. Learn his bent. Know which way she leans. Know your child, and love him with what you know. And when she is old, she will know who she is.

I read recently that the three primary pursuits of young people are pleasure, loyalty, and adventure. I assert these are perhaps the deepest longings for adults as well. We want to feel good, we want someone to stand beside us, and we want to avoid boredom. In themselves they're not lofty goals but not bad or unhealthy either. But if left unfulfilled, we may become even more desperate to attain them, and desperation is usually the root of poor health. And so, as the single mom of two boys, I add this to my mental check-list of things to consider.

Testosterone is such a foreign entity to me, and yet it is a far greater presence in our home than the estrogen counterpart. And I must somehow aim to channel these longings of theirs in ways that will gird them in strength, equip them to be faithful and true, and show them that what they want most is here at home. They don't have to go looking somewhere else, somewhere that could lead them entirely off course.

So I begin with adventure. That seems the easiest of the three. I choose to plan fun for the three of us, to show them that this trio is a fun place to belong. We can have fun, and they're welcome to invite others to join us as they grow older, but they don't need to look very far to find fun, laughter, and adventure. It lives in our home.

I can say yes until there's a reason to say no. "Sure, kiddo, give it a shot. If you think you can do it, give it a go." And perhaps this leaning toward yes will encourage them to one day answer the still, small voice that prompts them to do something great with their lives, something bigger than they are, something that started as an idea. The courage to say yes.

So then I look at loyalty. They're hungry for someone to stand by them, no matter what. Young people who do not find this in their home—in the inner city but also in affluent suburbs—find themselves instead looking for lasting affinity in other circles.

They could spend their lives spinning from one anchor to another, looking for anything to remain secure in the name of loyalty.

And so today I can aim to demonstrate what loyalty looks like. Model it. Show them "I am always here when you need me, but you do not always need me." There is a balance between loyalty and dependence, and it can be found—even if you must find it anew each day.

And then, that last one: pleasure. They're going to look for it, for what feels good, what matters most and offers the greatest high on any level. And so maybe my task is to show them that pleasure isn't the greatest good. That other things matter more, like love, joy, peace, patience, kindness, goodness, faithfulness, gentleness, and self-control.

Pleasure didn't make the list.

And if that means they don't get a Popsicle with every meal, well, then maybe that's the seed of the root of contentment.

If I wait until later to teach these things, I might miss my window. They might start looking before they even know what they're hungry for.

Okay, guys. Let's pursue some adventure, loyalty, and pleasure. Let's start right here.

epilogue

Dear Tucker and Tyler,

My goodness, I love you.

Tucker, I love your careful, linear thinking, your problem solving, and your great ideas. I love the freckles on your nose, the cowlick that matches mine, and your sturdy little body that is solid as a rock. I love how gentle you are with children, how careful you are with your brother, and how eager you are to try new things. I love that you can make me think. I love your thankful spirit. I love your caution and your humor, and I love the budding character that is beginning to take root. May you forever be kind, confident, and careful, my precious firstborn.

You are one great kid.

Tyler, I love your silly, random thoughts, your mind that never, ever stops going. I love that you make me laugh every single day. I love your ideas, your jokes, your tricks, and your fearlessness. I love that you love people, that you're ready for a party, that your hypersocial tendencies can only come from me. I love that you love books. I love the freckles on your nose, your sweeping eyelashes, your straight red hair, that cowlick that matches mine, and those irresistible dimples. I love that nothing ever slows you down. May you always be so resilient and courageous, my sweet second boy.

You are one great kid.

I love learning about you both.

I know I could never pray quite enough for you, and the thought of asking God for all the things I desire for you nearly paralyzes me and my prayer life. Still, I'm absolutely sure I'll spend the rest of my life trying.

You are the best things that ever, ever happened to me. I wouldn't trade you for all the little girls in the world, and I wouldn't trade a single day with you for a million days with anyone else.

I wonder sometimes what you'll remember about all this. I wonder what you will remember about our weekends, when you slept on the floor in my room after we finished watching a movie together, when we turned off all the lights but I kept the music streaming through the TV and you could see the glow of my laptop and hear the click of my fingers on the keys, and you knew I was thinking and writing and creating while I hummed my melodies. I listened to you while you listened to me, until I was the only one listening to your sleeping breaths. I wonder what you'll remember about these weekends, these Saturday nights. This life we've made for ourselves. I hope you'll remember love upon love upon love.

I could never possibly tell you how much you matter, but I'm absolutely sure I'll spend the rest of my life trying.

You know what, you guys? I think we're doing this. I think we're going to make it.

Eskimo kisses and big bear hugs,

Mom

acknowledgments

Sometimes when I'm writing, I feel like a preschooler negotiating what's left of her dinner. At times I am chewing and swallowing as fast as I can since it's all so delicious and I feel so privileged to have a seat at the table. Sometimes my creative well has run dry, and I'm just playing with my food without really any idea what else I can possibly do with the carrots and peas. The people who sit with me in this space are the real heroes.

I thank my mom and dad for making everything—*everything*—more fun. If you weren't already my mentors and friends, I'd be out of my mind looking for ways to know you and learn from you.

I thank my therapist, Jana, for shining your flashlight into my cave and believing in the girl hiding in the shadows.

I thank my agent, Greg, and his wife, Becky, for giving me an honorary PhD in hope.

I thank Bruce, my editor, the true archaeologist who finds the goodness in the mess.

I thank the servers at Chili's who let me camp out at a table and write until every single one of my batteries dies, both physically and metaphorically. You nourish me with chips, salsa, and Diet Cokes with lime.

I thank the sea of readers, the invisible you who listen to my stories as I try to make sense of it all. You keep me writing.

about the author

TRICIA LOTT WILLIFORD lives in Denver with her two sons, the athlete and the artist. Right this moment she is probably doodling in the margins of an overdue library book.